THE FEDERALISTS

Realists or Ideologues?

PROBLEMS IN AMERICAN CIVILIZATION

THE FEDERALISTS

Realists or Ideologues?

EDITED WITH AN INTRODUCTION BY
George Athan Billias
CLARK UNIVERSITY

D. C. HEATH AND COMPANY
Lexington, Massachusetts

CONTENTS

II. CONTROVERSY AMONG HISTORIANS

INTRODUCTION

WHAT manner of men were the Federalists of the 1790's? Were they hardheaded realists solely concerned with their own economic self-interests? Or were they high-minded ideologues intent upon promoting the public interest —not only in the sense of America's material prosperity but of its moral well-being? Were they shrewd politicians, utterly realistic in the goals that they sought and the policies they pursued? Or were they visionary men, whose aims could never be realized and whose policies were totally impractical? Those who studied the Federalists often have come to conflicting conclusions when answering such questions.

One group of political participants of the period and some scholars of later eras pictured the Federalists as political realists. To them the Federalists were self-interested, materialistic, and pragmatic —men whose ideas and actions were rooted in the recognition that a struggle for power was taking place in American society, who adopted measures mostly to protect their economic interests, and whose policies in political matters were practical and flexible. Seen in this light, the Federalists were usually identified by their adherence to a set of specific policies and goals—of removing the central government from control of the people for the purpose of protecting wealthy economic interests against the dangers of popularly-dominated state legislatures —of building an economic system that favored commerce, manufacturing, and finance at the expense of agriculture— and of following a pro-British foreign policy in order to advance America's commercial interests.

But a second group of contemporaries and certain subsequent historians saw the Federalists from a diametrically opposite point of view and described them as ideologues—men who were public-spirited, moralistic, and doctrinaire. To this group, the Federalists' aims appeared utterly unselfish and completely idealistic—of forming a government based on merit so that Americans might benefit from the virtue, wisdom, and prudence of society's natural leaders—of strengthening the central government to promote public prosperity and to safeguard public liberty against foreign invaders or potential domestic tyrants—of fostering commerce, manufacturing, and finance as a means to economic self-sufficiency and national security—and of pursuing a pro-British foreign policy in the belief that the future of America and of Western civilization itself depended upon an English victory over revolutionary France. Paradoxically, both groups arrived at their respective positions in this realist-ideologue dichotomy after examining the same set of Federalist principles, programs, and politicians.

Since the turn of the twentieth century, the majority of American historians have tended to view the Federalists as realists. Reading the policies and opinions expressed by the Federalist leaders —Washington, Hamilton, and John Adams at the national level; Fisher Ames, Timothy Pickering and George Cabot of the so-called "Essex Junto" in New England; John Jay and Rufus King in New York; and John Marshall, Charles C. Pinckney, and Robert G. Harper in the South—many modern-day scholars from Charles A. Beard to the present praised these men as pragmatic politicians. The Federalists, such historians said, carefully constructed their concept of a republican form of government upon a shrewd appraisal of human nature in general and the American national character in particular. This realist interpretation—as it may be called— generally characterized the Federalists in socio-economic terms. They were considered members of the conservative aristocratic class whose interests lay in financial, commercial, manufacturing, and speculative enterprises; the Jeffersonian Republicans, on the other hand, were depicted as representing the more democratic, agrarian interests.

The Federalists, according to this realist interpretation, showed their pragmatism by setting up a strong central government. In doing so, they demonstrated they had little faith in human nature or in the idea of undiluted democracy. To staff the government they turned to the nation's natural leaders—"the rich and well-born." Anxious to protect private property, they advocated the stake-in-society principle and insisted that only those with somewhat substantial economic holdings should be given the right to vote and to run for office. Yet they were practical enough not to become aristocratic tyrants. Recognizing the temper of the American people, they built their system of government upon the principle of the consent of the governed.

This view also portrayed the Federalists as anti-democrats—men fearful of a possible tyranny or uprising on the part of the masses. To support this image of the Federalists, Hamilton's dictum, "The people are turbulent and changing, they seldom judge or determine right," was cited. John Jay's observation likewise was quoted: "The mass of men are neither wise nor good, and virtue, like the other resources of a country, can only be drawn to a point and exerted by . . . a strong government ably administered." And much was made of the fact that Charles Pinckney, a Federalist in his early days, proposed that no one become President who was not worth at least $100,000.

Federalist domestic policies, the realist interpretation continued, were aimed at placing the wealthy class in secure control of the central government. Hamilton's program for funding the national debt reflected a key article of faith in the Federalist creed: to create a loyal governing class among men of substance by advocating policies which openly favored their economic interests. His plans for a national bank, a national tariff, and his broad constructionist view of the Constitution were all part of the same pattern —to provide benefits to the nation's businessmen in the belief that no government could long endure unless it had the confidence and support of the propertied class. Historians holding this view conceded, however, that Hamilton's policies backfired in one sense: the programs designed to unite the nation behind the Federalists tended to produce just the opposite effect—they gave rise to Jeffersonian Republican opposition instead.

In evaluating Federalist foreign policy, advocates of this position pointed to a similar strain of realism. It was said that the two Federalist presidents—Washington and Adams—were acutely conscious of America's weakness; both felt that the new nation needed time to grow strong. Therefore, the two presidents and their advisors adopted a flexible and pragmatic approach in handling the problems facing America in world affairs. When the outbreak of hostilities in 1793 divided Europe into two warring camps, Washington immediately issued his Neutrality Proclamation. Hamilton, traditionally pro-British and fearful of the effect a war with the former mother country might have on his financial policies, actually went so far as to leak secret information to England to help bring about the signing of Jay's treaty. Washington's famous Farewell Address not only articulated a central principle in America's foreign policy—that of isolation from Europe—but warned also against the dangerous political divisions which might be created within the country by disagreements over diplomacy. John Adams, continuing America's realistic diplomatic policy of political isolation from Europe, supposedly severed the last formal tie binding the New World to the Old by terminating the 1778 Franco-American alliance in 1800.

The view of the Federalists as ideologues—a second line of interpretation—developed alongside that which regarded them as realists. This approach usually categorized the Federalists in ideological and intellectual terms—as men bound together by a set of common beliefs, values, and ideas—rather than as members of an economic class with similar self-interests. Within this context the Federalists were characterized as ideologues who based their political behavior upon a rather rigid conception of American society as they thought it *ought* to be. Taking a dim view of human nature, they held that if men were fit to govern themselves at all it must be only under strict conditions imposed upon them by society and government. The Federalists became so doctrinaire in their outlook, it was said, that they failed to cope with the problem of power on realistic terms; they remained inflexibly faithful to their fixed political principles despite changes in public opinion.

This same interpretation depicted many Federalists as firm believers in the idea of a deferential society—a hierarchical social order based upon a system of deference. In such a society all mankind was naturally divided into two groups— natural leaders who constituted an elite, and the plain people who continually elected their leaders from an aristocracy of merit because of ingrained habits of subordination. The elite were taught to possess a sense of responsibility, to have a genuine regard for the well-being of their inferiors, and to lead society to the best of their abilities. The plain people, on their part, were taught from birth to be obedient, to confer the powers of government upon their superiors, and to recognize it was in their best interests to be led by their betters. Federalists of this mind assumed a natural inequality among men and looked to the system of deference to provide the cement to hold society together.

This Federalist ideal of a deferential society rested upon three main premises. First, aware of the depravities of human nature, the Federalists were pessimistic about the ability of men in general to govern themselves wisely. Only the elite —by virtue of their birth, training, talent, wealth, and social station—could be trusted to protect private property and human rights. Secondly, social stability could best be achieved if the plain people *willingly* consented to be ruled by their betters. Within a deferential society there was likely to be less social conflict from classes, factions, or parties contending for power. Thirdly, that a ruling elite was more apt to safeguard the interests of society as a whole. Consistent with their view of man's innate selfish nature and uncontrollable passions, the Federalists believed that government was the instrument created by society to protect men from one another. Government would succeed, however, only if rigid controls were imposed upon the people, and the private interests and liberties of the individual were subordinated to the public good.

The Jeffersonian Republicans, the ideologue interpretation continued, held different ideas about human nature and the purposes of government. Taking a more optimistic view, they assumed that men were by nature inclined to be rational and good. Once men were freed from the bonds of ignorance and repression, reason would inevitably triumph over passion and good over evil. Most Jeffersonian Republicans, it was said, believed that the people in the aggregate were trustworthy; the majority of men, under proper conditions, therefore, could govern themselves wisely. Having a greater trust in mankind, the Republicans believed that an informed and educated electorate, under normal circumstances, would vote into office the most talented and intelligent men in society. Two corollaries presumably arose from such views of a responsible electorate and intelligent leaders: the Jeffersonians believed in minimum rather than maximum government; and they tended to think more in terms of protecting the rights and liberties of the individual than those of society. Hence, this line of interpretation concluded, the more democratic-minded Americans became Jeffersonians, and when the idea of a deferential society went into decline the Republicans swept into power in 1800.

The Federalist foreign policy, in keeping with this version, was likewise held to be more idealistic in nature. Both Federalists and Republicans dreamed of the day when America would become a great world power, commanding the respect of other nations. To reach this goal, however, the Federalists believed more deeply than their opponents that it was necessary for the country to set its internal affairs in order first. By reducing tensions between social classes, calming fears regarding states' rights, and restoring financial stability at home, America's prestige would be enhanced abroad. Devoted to the ideal of public order, moreover, the Federalists supposedly looked to conservative England rather than radical France as their model. To many of them the French Revolution raised hysterical fears of mob rule, atheism, and Jacobinism in America. When war broke out in Europe in the 1790's, they favored Britain in the belief that the infant nation might not survive if the forces of anarchy and disorder in France were loosed upon the rest of the Western world. To sum up, the ideologue interpretation held that Federalists' goals in both domestic and foreign affairs were consonant with the same end: to build a strong and stable nation-state along idealistic lines.

The contemporary documents presented in the first half of this book illustrate the problem of trying to determine whether the Federalists were realists or ideologues. Take, for example, the first two selections—Hamilton's "First Report on the Public Credit" and his "Report on Manufactures." To the Federalists, economic policy was, perhaps, the single most important problem facing the new nation. Hamilton's proposal—to restore confidence in America's credit by having the central government assume responsibility for both state and federal debts at face value, and to raise an adequate public revenue to fund such debts—was sound. But what was the motivation behind Hamilton's funding and assumption program? Was it his purpose to enrich the upper class—to show greater concern for private profits than the public interest? Or was he thinking more of the nation's welfare—acting out of a belief that the central government could not survive unless it secured the support of the wealthy class? When Hamilton stressed the importance of promoting manufacturing in his second report, did he do so out of a desire to make America an industrial rather than an agricultural country in line with his dream of building a strong and prosperous nation? Or was he seeking only to find another way to bind the loyalties of well-to-do manufacturers to the national government?

The same kinds of questions can be raised about the next selection—Washington's Farewell Address. Written with Hamilton's help to announce Washington's retirement, the message could be read two ways. Seen from the perspective of the ideologue interpretation, the Address could be seen as an idealistic document: a piece of sage advice by the father of his country to the people and their posterity to guard against the twin dangers of factionalism and sectionalism which might permit foreign nations to intrude upon America's domestic affairs. Viewed in a more partisan light, however, the message could be read as a party tract—one whose main purpose was to influence the outcome of the 1796 election. What did Washington and Hamilton have in mind when they wrote the Address? Were they thinking in terms of the national interest—proposing principles for a long-range foreign policy for America? Or were they considering only short-term self-interest—seeking to insure the re-election of the Federalists and to frustrate the French who were attempting to meddle in America's presidential campaign?

Even the Federalists themselves disagreed about whether they were realists or ideologues, as may be seen in the next three selections by Fisher Ames and Robert G. Harper. Ames claimed it took an act of faith on the part of the Federalists to establish a republican form of government in the 1790's. Republics had been notoriously unstable throughout history, he pointed out; such governments could exist only as long as their leaders and citizens remained virtuous and moral. Assuming this to be true of America's statesmen and citizenry, the Federalists had set up a republic—only to be undermined by the demagogic Jeffersonian Republican "faction" in the election of 1800. In the first of his selections, Ames pointed to Washington as an example of the virtuous and moral leader the Federalists had provided. But the Federalists, Ames concluded bitterly in his second selection, had been extreme idealists; they had mistakenly depended upon the "supposed existence of public virtue, and on the permanency of public morals" to sustain themselves in power. Robert G. Harper, a Republican-turned-

Federalist, took an opposite point of view: he listed a series of practical political maxims employed by members of his adopted party that had enabled the Federalists, in his judgment, to provide a much more realistic leadership than their opponents.

Since the Federalists disagreed about whether they were realists or ideologues, it is not surprising to find their political opponents divided on the same question. The next three selections were written by persons who were, or would become, Jeffersonian Republicans—Mercy Otis Warren and James Madison. In her history published in 1805, Mrs. Warren described Washington in idealistic terms, picturing him as a great man who stood above petty political partisanship and one who governed unselfishly in the best interests of all the people. Madison, on the other hand, as early as 1792 identified certain of Washington's followers as "Anti-republicans." These men, Madison claimed in the next two selections, were serving their own selfish interests rather than trying to uphold the ideals of the republican form of government.

In the election of 1800, the controversy concerning the true nature of the Federalist party became more pronounced. Why had the Federalists failed, contemporaries asked? Had the party lost on practical grounds because it backed unwise policies: favoring financial and commercial interests over agrarian groups, oppressing its allegedly treasonous opponents with the Alien and Sedition Acts, carrying on the Quasi-War with France, and increasing taxes to pay for military preparations? Had the party lost because of faulty political tactics: splitting itself into two wings—one led by Hamilton and the other by Adams— at the time of the election? Or had the Federalists lost because they had been too idealistic? Were they ideologues too strongly committeed to the ideal of a society ruled by an elite? Did the Federalists stubbornly cling to their convictions at a time when the concept of a deferential society was collapsing before their eyes as the more democratic ideas of the Jeffersonian Republicans gained

primacy among the people?

Political participants of the period provided evidence to support both points of view. Thomas Jefferson—showing himself to be a shrewd political observer in the next selection—predicted as far back as the mid-1790's that the Federalists would go down to defeat because they were backing unpopular policies. In another letter written in 1802, Jefferson concluded that the Federalists were routed in 1800 primarily as the result of a whole host of political blunders. But Robert Troup, a Federalist writing just prior to the election of 1800, presented a different picture and revealed the rather idealistic world view held by many of the members of his party. Troup predicted that America would face slave uprisings and domestic insurrections if his party lost. Only the Federalist elite— the friends of law and order, he implied —were capable of maintaining control within the country.

The two conflicting views of the Federalists taken by themselves and their contemporaries continued down through the years and became the basis for much of the current historiographical controversy. Whether dealing with Federalist leaders or the Federalist party, many of the present-day historians tended to view them within the context of a realist-ideologue dichotomy—as the succeeding selections show. Some modern scholars, for example, used Hamilton as the focus of the problem. Richard B. Morris in his article saw him as a supreme realist—an advocate of power politics in both domestic and foreign affairs. Cecelia M. Kenyon, in her penetrating essay, took an opposite point of view; Hamilton's political ideas were postulated on the assumption that men were idealistic, she claimed, and he believed that men could perceive the public good and would act on that basis. Current scholars had a similar disagreement in their estimates of Washington. Alexander De Conde pictured Washington as a highly partisan President whose Farewell Address was motivated by practical ends—to gain an immediate political advantage in the election of 1796. David H. Fischer, on the other hand, presented Washington as a Federalist politician, but one who was an ideologue. Washington's political actions, according to Fischer, were based on three fixed principles: he was an elitist whose politics were premised upon the concept of a deferential society; a collectivist who took a corporate view of society; and a man who believed that government was basically a moral, not a political, problem.

In evaluating the Federalist party, modern scholars likewise have approached the problem from completely different perspectives. Manning Dauer, defining the political parties in the 1790's in socio-economic terms, concluded in his selection that the commercial farmers who exported surplus crops invariably became Federalists. Subsistence farmers, on the other hand, tended to join the Jeffersonian Republican ranks. The commercial farmers held the balance of power within the country, Dauer suggested, and John Adams, being a political realist, recognized this fact and did everything he could to gain their support. Lawrence S. Kaplan, on the other hand, identified the Federalists as idealists and claimed that the party committed "political suicide" as its members became rigid ideologues. The Federalists, Kaplan said, refused to modify their principles; they failed to adjust their ideology to accommodate the rising tide of democratic ideas that characterized the new political age.

How was it possible, the student of history may ask, for contemporary observers and modern scholars to arrive at such contradictory conclusions? The answer lies, perhaps, in the fact that many of those who studied the Federalists in the past have insisted upon viewing them in mutually exclusive categories—as being either realists or ideologues. It may well be, however, that the Federalists were both realists and ideologues at one and the same time: both self-interested and public-spirited, materialistic and moralistic, pragmatic and doctrinaire. In this, they shared the dilemma that the American people have faced throughout their history—that of resolving the conflict and balancing the tension between their realism and idealism.

The American people never have given widespread political support to parties that were wholly idealistic in nature. On the other hand, neither have we been able to escape our ideological affection for those principles expressed in the Declaration of Independence. No political party failing to render allegiance to these principles has ever been able to secure broad political backing. Thus, the problem confronting the Federalists in the 1790's—that of reconciling realism and idealism—continues to challenge America's political parties to this day.

THE CONFLICT OF OPINION

Were the Federalists realistic or idealistic?

> Regulating its conduct by these maxims, the government of the United States under the direction of the Federalists, with Washington and afterwards Adams at their head, has preserved the nation in peace, through the most general and the most furious war that has afflicted the world in modern times.
>
> —ROBERT GOODLOE HARPER

> We have been the visionary men, who have believed, as many have, that mere Paper Constitutions, without those moral and political habits and opinions, which alone give solidity and support to any Government, would be sufficient to protect and preserve the equal Rights of the weak against the strong, of the honest agt. the dishonest, of the wise and faithful friends of free Govt. against the wicked and ambitious men, who disregard every thing that stands in the way of their criminal desires.
>
> —RUFUS KING

Why did the Federalists lose at the polls?

> The cause assigned by the Federalists for their failure is, that the election day was rainy, and that a large number of strong Federal votes from the remotest part of the town was lost by non-attendance. This is one of a thousand proofs how a large portion of Federalism is a mere fair-weather principle, too weak to overcome a shower of rain. It shows the degree of dependence that can be placed upon such friends. As a party, their adversaries are more sure, and more earnest.
>
> —JOHN QUINCY ADAMS

> They say we lied them out of power, and openly avow they will do the same by us. But it was not lies or argument on our part which dethroned them, but their own foolish acts, sedition laws, alien laws, taxes, extravagance & heresies.
>
> —THOMAS JEFFERSON

What were the chances of a Federalist comeback after 1800?

> We poor fallen Federalists are indulging our expectation that the sun of Federalism is beginning to rise again. In Massachusetts and Connecticut larger majorities for the Federalists appeared at the State elections than in those of last year.
>
> —ROBERT TROUP

> Among Federalists old errors are not cured. They also continue to dream though not so preposterously as their opponent. All will be very well (say they) when the power once more gets into Federal hands. The people convinced by experience of their error will repose a *permanent* confidence in good men. *Risum teneatis?* [Can you keep from laughing?]
>
> —ALEXANDER HAMILTON

Was Alexander Hamilton a realist?

Hamilton's remarkable grasp of national interest was evident in the direction he gave to the foreign policy of the Washington administration. He was a realist.

—RICHARD B. MORRIS

Hamilton was never able to reconcile his political ideal with his announced view of political reality; and . . . as a result, his political theory is confused, contradictory, and basically unrealistic.

—CECELIA M. KENYON

I. CONTROVERSY AMONG CONTEMPORARIES

Alexander Hamilton

REPORT ON THE PUBLIC CREDIT

Alexander Hamilton, appointed secretary of the treasury by Washington, considered his position comparable to that of England's prime minister. Charged with submitting a budget, he outlined instead a comprehensive plan to strengthen the central government. His report, written in 1790, is a revealing document because it contains key parts of the Federalist program. In practical terms his report presented the guidelines on which Hamilton hoped to base the economic policies of the new government. But more important than being a blueprint for fiscal reform, the document represented the *raison d'etre* for Hamilton's program. His idea for wooing the monied class to the central government, on the grounds that the interests of the upper class were inseparable from those of the rest of society as a whole, has been called both idealistic and realistic. Was this idea based upon a philosophy similar to Rousseau's concept of the "general will"? Or was it simply a crude appeal to the self-interest of the upper class?

THE Secretary of the Treasury, in obedience to the resolution of the House of Representatives of the twenty-first day of September last, has, during the recess of Congress, applied himself to the consideration of a proper plan for the support of the public credit, with all the attention which was due to the authority of the House, and to the magnitude of the object.

In the discharge of this duty, he has felt, in no small degree, the anxieties which naturally flow from a just estimate of the difficulty of the task, from a well founded diffidence of his own qualifications for executing it with success, and from a deep and solemn conviction of the momentous nature of the truth contained in the resolution under which his investigations have been conducted, "That an adequate provision for the support of the public credit is a matter of high importance to the honor and prosperity of the United States."

With an ardent desire that his well meant endeavors may be conducive to the real advantage of the nation, and with the utmost deference to the superior judgment of the House, he now respectfully submits the result of his inquiries and reflections to their indulgent construction.

In the opinion of the Secretary, the wisdom of the House, in giving their explicit sanction to the proposition which has been stated, cannot but be applauded by all who will seriously consider and trace, through their obvious consequences, these plain and undeniable truths:

That exigencies are to be expected to occur, in the affairs of nations, in which there will be a necessity for borrowing.

That loans in times of public danger, especially from foreign war, are found an indispensable resource, even to the wealthiest of them.

And that, in a country which, like

From John C. Hamilton, ed., *Works of Alexander Hamilton* (New York, 1850–1851), Vol. III, pp. 1–16, 44–45.

this, is possessed of little active wealth, or, in other words, little moneyed capital, the necessity for that resource must, in such emergencies, be proportionably urgent.

And as, on the one hand, the necessity for borrowing, in particular emergencies, cannot be doubted, so, on the other, it is equally evident, that, to be able to borrow upon good terms, it is essential that the credit of a nation should be well established.

For, when the credit of a country is in any degree questionable, it never fails to give an extravagant premium, in one shape or another, upon all the loans it has occasion to make. Nor does the evil end here; the same disadvantage must be sustained upon whatever is to be bought on terms of future payment.

From this constant necessity of borrowing and buying dear, it is easy to conceive how immensely the expenses of a nation, in a course of time, will be augmented by an unsound state of the public credit.

To attempt to enumerate the complicated variety of mischiefs in the whole system of the social economy, which proceed from a neglect of the maxims that uphold public credit, and justify the solicitude manifested by the House on this point, would be an improper intrusion on their time and patience.

In so strong a light, nevertheless, do they appear to the Secretary, that, on their due observance, at the present critical juncture, materially depends, in his judgment, the individual and aggregate prosperity of the citizens of the United States; their relief from the embarrassments they now experience; their character as a people; the cause of good government.

If the maintenance of public credit, then, be truly so important, the next inquiry which suggests itself is, By what means is it to be effected? The ready answer to which question is, by good faith; by a punctual performance of contracts. States, like individuals, who observe their engagements, are respected and trusted, while the reverse is the fate of those who pursue an opposite conduct.

Every breach of the public engagements, whether from choice or necessity, is, in different degrees, hurtful to public credit. When such a necessity does truly exist, the evils of it are only to be palliated by a scrupulous attention, on the part of the Government, to carry the violation no further than the necessity absolutely requires, and to manifest, if the nature of the case admit of it, a sincere disposition to make reparation whenever circumstances shall permit. But, with every possible mitigation, credit must suffer, and numerous mischiefs ensue. It is, therefore, highly important, when an appearance of necessity seems to press upon the public councils, that they should examine well its reality, and be perfectly assured that there is no method of escaping from it, before they yield to its suggestions. For, though it cannot safely be affirmed that occasions have never existed, or may not exist, in which violations of the public faith, in this respect, are inevitable; yet there is great reason to believe, that they exist far less frequently than precedents indicate, and are oftenest either pretended, through levity or want of firmness; or supposed through want of knowledge. Expedients often have been devised to effect, consistently with good faith, what has been done in contravention of it. Those who are most commonly creditors of a nation, are, generally speaking, enlightened men; and there are signal examples to warrant a conclusion, that, when a candid and fair appeal is made to them, they will understand their true interest too well to refuse their concurrence in such modifications of their claims as any real necessity may demand.

While the observance of that good faith, which is the basis of public credit, is recommended by the strongest inducements of political expediency, it is enforced by considerations of still greater authority. There are arguments for it which rest on the immutable principles of moral obligation. And in proportion as the mind is disposed to contemplate, in the order of Providence, an intimate connection between public virtue and public happiness, will be its repugnancy to a violation of those principles.

This reflection derives additional

strength from the nature of the debt of the United States. It was the price of liberty. The faith of America has been repeatedly pledged for it, and with solemnities that give peculiar force to the obligation. There is, indeed, reason to regret that it has not hitherto been kept; that the necessities of the war, conspiring with inexperience in the subjects of finance, produced direct infractions; and that the subsequent period has been a continued scene of negative violation or non-compliance. But a diminution of this regret arises from the reflection, that the last seven years have exhibited an earnest and uniform effort, on the part of the Government of the Union, to retrieve the national credit, by doing justice to the creditors of the nation; and that the embarrassments of a defective constitution, which defeated this laudable effort, have ceased.

From this evidence of a favorable disposition given by the former Government, the institution of a new one, clothed with powers competent to calling forth the resources of the community, has excited correspondent expectations. A general belief accordingly prevails, that the credit of the United States will quickly be established on the firm foundation of an effectual provision for the existing debt. The influence which this has had at home, is witnessed by the rapid increase that has taken place in the market value of the public securities. From January to November, they rose thirty-three and a third per cent.; and, from that period to this time, they have risen fifty per cent. more; and the intelligence from abroad announces effects proportionably favorable to our national credit and consequence.

It cannot but merit particular attention, that, among ourselves, the most enlightened friends of good government are those whose expectations are the highest.

To justify and preserve their confidence; to promote the increasing respectability of the American name; to answer the calls of justice; to restore landed property to its due value; to furnish new resources, both to agriculture and commerce; to cement more closely the union of the States; to add to their security against foreign attack; to establish public order on the basis of an upright and liberal policy;—these are the great and invaluable ends to be secured by a proper and adequate provision, at the present period, for the support of public credit.

To this provision we are invited, not only by the general considerations which have been noticed, but by others of a more particular nature. It will procure, to every class of the community, some important advantages, and remove some no less important disadvantages.

The advantage to the public creditors, from the increased value of that part of their property which constitutes the public debt, needs no explanation.

But there is a consequence of this, less obvious, though not less true, in which every other citizen is interested. It is a well known fact, that, in countries in which the national debt is properly funded, and an object of established confidence, it answers most of the purposes of money. Transfers of stock or public debt, are there equivalent to payments in specie; or, in other words, stock, in the principal transactions of business, passes current as specie. The same thing would, in all probability, happen here under the like circumstances.

The benefits of this are various and obvious:

First. Trade is extended by it, because there is a larger capital to carry it on, and the merchant can, at the same time, afford to trade for smaller profits; as his stock, which, when unemployed, brings him in an interest from the Government, serves him also as money when he has a call for it in his commercial operations.

Secondly. Agriculture and manufactures are also promoted by it, for the like reason, that more capital can be commanded to be employed in both; and because the merchant, whose enterprise in foreign trade gives to them activity and extension, has greater means for enterprise.

Thirdly. The interest of money will be lowered by it; for this is always in a ratio to the quantity of money, and to the quickness of circulation. This circumstance will enable both the public and individuals to borrow on easier and cheaper terms.

And from the combination of these effects, additional aids will be furnished to labor, to industry, and to arts of every kind. But these good effects of a public debt are only to be looked for, when, by being well funded, it has acquired an adequate and stable value; till then, it has rather a contrary tendency. The fluctuation and insecurity incident to it, in an unfunded state, render it a mere commodity, and a precarious one. As such, being only an object of occasional and particular speculation, all the money applied to it is so much diverted from the more useful channels of circulation, for which the thing itself affords no substitute; so that, in fact, one serious inconvenience of an unfunded debt is, that it contributes to the scarcity of money.

This distinction, which has been little if at all attended to, is of the greatest moment; it involves a question immediately interesting to every part of the community, which is no other than this: Whether the public debt, by a provision for it on true principles, shall be rendered a substitute for money; or whether, by being left as it is, or by being provided for in such a manner as will wound those principles, and destroy confidence, it shall be suffered to continue as it is, a pernicious drain of our cash from the channels of productive industry?

The effect which the funding of the public debt, on right principles, would have upon landed property, is one of the circumstances attending such an arrangement, which has been least adverted to, though it deserves the most particular attention. The present depreciated state of that species of property is a serious calamity. The value of cultivated lands, in most of the States, has fallen, since the Revolution, from twenty five to fifty per cent. In those further south, the decrease is still more considerable. Indeed, if the representations continually received from that quarter may be credited, lands there will command no price which may not be deemed an almost total sacrifice. This decrease in the value of lands, ought, in a great measure, to be attributed to the scarcity of money; consequently, whatever produces an augmentation of the moneyed capital of the country, must have a proportional effect in raising that value. The beneficial tendency of a funded debt, in this respect, has been manifested by the most decisive experience in Great Britain.

The proprietors of lands would not only feel the benefit of this increase in the value of their property, and of a more prompt and better sale, when they had occasion to sell, but the necessity of selling would be itself greatly diminished. As the same cause would contribute to the facility of loans, there is reason to believe that such of them as are indebted, would be able, through that resource, to satisfy their more urgent creditors.

It ought not, however, to be expected, that the advantages described as likely to result from funding the public debt, would be instantaneous. It might require some time to bring the value of stock to its natural level, and to attach to it that fixed confidence which is necessary to its quality as money. Yet the late rapid rise of the public securities encourages an expectation that the progress of stock, to the desirable point, will be much more expeditious than could have been foreseen. And as, in the mean time, it will be increasing in value, there is room to conclude that it will, from the outset, answer many of the purposes in contemplation. Particularly, it seems to be probable, that from creditors, who are not themselves necessitous, it will early meet with a ready reception in payment of debts, at its current price.

Having now taken a concise view of the inducements to a proper provision for the public debt, the next inquiry which presents itself is, What ought to be the nature of such a provision? This requires some preliminary discussions.

It is agreed, on all hands, that that part of the debt which has been contracted abroad, and is denominated the foreign debt, ought to be provided for according to the precise terms of the contracts relating to it. The discussions which can arise, therefore, will have reference essentially to the domestic part of it, or to that which has been contracted at home. It is to be regretted that there is not the same unanimity of sentiment on this part as on the other.

The Secretary has too much deference for the opinions of every part of the community, not to have observed one, which has more than once made its appearance in the public prints, and which is occasionally to be met with in conversation. It involves this question: Whether a discrimination ought not to be made between original holders of the public securities, and present possessors, by purchase? Those who advocate a discrimination, are for making a full provision for the securities of the former at their nominal value; but contend that the latter ought to receive no more than the cost to them, and the interest. And the idea is sometimes suggested, of making good the difference to the primitive possessor.

In favor of this scheme, it is alleged, that it would be unreasonable to pay twenty shillings in the pound, to one who had not given more for it than three or four. And it is added, that it would be hard to aggravate the misfortune of the first owner, who, probably, through necessity, parted with his property at so great a loss, by obliging him to contribute to the profit of the person who had speculated on his distresses.

The Secretary, after the most mature reflection on the force of this argument, is induced to reject the doctrine it contains, as equally unjust and impolitic; as highly injurious, even to the original holders of public securities; as ruinous to public credit.

It is inconsistent with justice, because, in the first place, it is a breach of contract—a violation of the rights of a fair purchaser.

The nature of the contract, in its origin, is, that the public will pay the sum expressed in the security, to the first holder or his assignee. The intent in making the security assignable, is, that the proprietor may be able to make use of his property, by selling it for as much as it may be worth in the market, and that the buyer may be safe in the purchase.

Every buyer, therefore, stands exactly in the place of the seller; has the same right with him to the identical sum expressed in the security; and, having acquired that right, by fair purchase, and in conformity to the original agreement and intention of the Government, his claim cannot be disputed without manifest injustice.

That he is to be considered as a fair purchaser, results from this: whatever necessity the seller may have been under, was occasioned by the Government, in not making a proper provision for its debts. The buyer had no agency in it, and therefore ought not to suffer. He is not even chargeable with having taken an undue advantage. He paid what the commodity was worth in the market, and took the risks of reimbursement upon himself. He, of course, gave a fair equivalent, and ought to reap the benefit of his hazard—a hazard which was far from inconsiderable, and which, perhaps, turned on little less than a revolution in government.

That the case of those who parted with their securities, from necessity, is a hard one, cannot be denied. But, whatever complaint of injury, or claim of redress, they may have, respects the Government solely. They have not only nothing to object to the persons who relieved their necessities, by giving them the current price of their property, but they are even under an implied condition to contribute to the reimbursement of those persons. They knew that, by the terms of the contract with themselves, the public were bound to pay to those to whom they should convey their title the sums stipulated to be paid to them; and that, as citizens of the United States, they were to bear their proportion of the contribution for that purpose. This, by the act of assignment, they tacitly engage to do; and, if they had an option, they could not, with integrity or good faith, refuse to do it, without the consent of those to whom they sold.

But, though many of the original holders sold from necessity, it does not follow that this was the case with all of them. It may well be supposed that some of them did it either through want of confidence in an eventual provision, or from the allurements of some profitable speculation. How shall these different classes be discriminated from each other? How shall it be ascertained, in any case, that the money which the original holder obtained for his security, was not more beneficial to him, than if he had held it to the present time, to avail himself of the provision which shall be made? How shall it be known whether, if the purchaser had employed his money in some other way, he would not be in a better situation than by having applied it in the purchase of securities, though he should now receive their full amount? And, if neither of these things can be known, how shall it be determined, whether a discrimination, independent of the breach of contract, would not do a real injury to purchasers; and, if it included a compensation to the primitive proprietors, would not give them an advantage to which they had no equitable pretension?

It may well be imagined, also, that there are not wanting instances, in which individuals, urged by a present necessity, parted with the securities received by them from the public, and shortly after replaced them with others, as an indemnity for their first loss. Shall they be deprived of the indemnity which they have endeavored to secure by so provident an arrangement?

Questions of this sort, on a close inspection, multiply themselves without end, and demonstrate the injustice of a discrimination, even on the most subtle calculations of equity, abstracted from the obligation of contract.

The difficulties, too, of regulating the details of a plan for that purpose, which would have even the semblance of equity, would be found immense. It may well be doubted, whether they would not be insurmountable, and replete with such absurd as well as inequitable consequences, as to disgust even the proposers of the measure.

As a specimen of its capricious operation, it will be sufficient to notice the effect it would have upon two persons, who may be supposed, two years ago, to have purchased, each, securities, at three shillings in the pound, and one of them to retain those bought by him, till the discrimination should take place; the other, to have parted with those bought by him, within a month past, at nine shillings. The former, who had had most confidence in the Government, would, in this case, only receive at the rate of three shillings, and the interest; while the latter, who had had less confidence, would receive for what cost him the same money, at the rate of nine shillings, and his representative, standing in his place, would be entitled to a like rate.

The impolicy of a discrimination results from two considerations: one, that it proceeds upon a principle destructive of that quality of the public debt, or the stock of the nation, which is essential to its capacity for answering the purposes of money, that is, the security of transfer; the other, that, as well on this account as because it includes a breach of faith, it renders property, in the funds, less valuable, consequently, induces lenders to demand a higher premium for what they lend, and produces every other inconvenience of a bad state of public credit.

It will be perceived, at first sight, that the transferable quality of stock is essential to its operation as money, and that this depends on the idea of complete security to the transferee, and a firm persuasion, that no distinction can, in any circumstances, be made between him and the original proprietor.

The precedent of an invasion of this fundamental principle, would, of course, tend to deprive the community of an advantage with which no temporary saving could bear the least comparison.

And it will as readily be perceived, that the same cause would operate a diminution of the value of stock in the hands of the first as well as of every other holder. The price which any man who should incline to purchase, would be willing to give for it, would be in a compound ratio to the immediate profit it afforded, and the chance of the continuance of his profit. If there was supposed to be any hazard of the latter, the risk would be taken into the calculation, and either there would be no purchase at all, or it would be at a proportionably less price.

For this diminution of the value of stock, every person who should be about to lend to the Government, would demand compensation, and would add to the actual difference between the nominal and the market value, an equivalent for the chance of greater decrease, which, in a precarious state of public credit, is always to be taken into the account. Every compensation of this sort, it is evident, would be an absolute loss to the Government.

In the preceding discussion of the impolicy of a discrimination, the injurious tendency of it to those who continue to be the holders of the securities they received from the Government, has been explained. Nothing need be added on this head, except that this is an additional and interesting light in which the injustice of the measure may be seen. It would not only divest present proprietors, by purchase, of the rights they had acquired under the sanction of public faith, but it would depreciate the property of the remaining original holders. It is equally unnecessary to add any thing to what has been already said, to demonstrate the fatal influence which the principle of discrimination would have on the public credit.

But there is still a point of view, in which it will appear perhaps even more exceptionable than in either of the former. It would be repugnant to an express provision of the Constitution of the United States. This provision is, that "all debts contracted, and engagements entered into, before the adoption of that Constitution, shall be as valid against the United States under it, as under the Confederation"; which amounts to a constitutional ratification of the contracts respecting the debt, in the state in which they existed under the Confederation. And, resorting to that standard, there can be no doubt that the rights of assignees and original holders must be considered as equal. In exploding thus fully the principle of discrimination, the Secretary is happy in reflecting, that he is only the advocate of what has been already sanctioned by the formal and express authority of the Government of the Union, in these emphatic terms: "The remaining class of creditors," says Congress, in their circular addressed to the States, of the 26th April, 1783, "is composed of such of our fellow-citizens as originally lent to the public the use of their funds, or have since manifested most confidence in their country, by receiving transfers from the lenders; and partly of those whose property has been either advanced or assumed for the public service. To discriminate the merits of these several descriptions of creditors, would be a task equally unnecessary and invidious. If the voice of humanity pleads more loudly in favor of some than of others, the voice of policy, no less than of justice, pleads in favor of all. A wise nation will never permit those who relieve the wants of their country, or who rely most on its faith, its firmness, and its resources, when either of them is distrusted, to suffer by the event."

The Secretary, concluding that a discrimination between the different classes of creditors of the United States cannot, with propriety, be made, proceeds to examine whether a difference ought to be permitted to remain between them and another description of public creditors —those of the States, individually. The Secretary, after mature reflection on this point, entertains a full conviction, that an assumption of the debts of the particular States by the Union, and a like provision for them, as for those of the Union, will be a measure of sound policy and substantial justice.

It would, in the opinion of the Secretary, contribute, in an eminent degree, to an orderly, stable, and satisfactory arrangement of the national finances. Admitting, as ought to be the case, that a provision must be made, in some way or other, for the entire debt, it will follow that no greater revenues will be required, whether that provision be made wholly by the United States, or partly by them, and partly by the States separately.

The principal question, then, must be, whether such a provision cannot be more conveniently and effectually made, by one general plan, issuing from one authority, than by different plans, originating in different authorities? In the first case, there can be no competition for resources; in the last, there must be such a competition. The consequences of this, without the greatest caution on both sides, might be interfering regulations, and thence, collision and confusion. Particular branches of industry might also be oppressed by it. The most productive objects of revenue are not numerous. Either these must be wholly engrossed by one side, which might lessen the efficacy of the provisions by the other, or both must have recourse to the same objects, in different modes, which might occasion an accumulation upon them, beyond what they could properly bear. If this should not happen, the caution requisite to avoiding it, would prevent the revenue's deriving the full benefit of each object. The danger of interference and of excess, would be apt to impose restraints very unfriendly to the complete command of those resources which are the most convenient, and to compel the having recourse to others, less eligible in themselves, and less agreeable to the community. The difficulty of an effectual command of the public resources, in case of separate provisions for the debt, may be seen in another, and, perhaps, more striking light. It would naturally happen that different States, from local considerations, would, in some instances, have recourse to different objects, in others to the same objects, in different degrees, for procuring the funds of which they stood in need. It is easy to conceive how this diversity would affect the aggregate revenue of the country. By the supposition, articles which yielded a full supply in some States, would yield nothing, or an insufficient product, in others. And hence, the public revenue would not derive the full benefit of those articles from State regulations; neither could the deficiencies be made good by those of the Union. It is a provision of the national Constitution, that "all duties, imposts, and excises, shall be uniform throughout the United States." And, as the General Government would be under a necessity, from motives of policy, of paying regard to the duty which may have been previously imposed upon any article, though but in a single State, it would be constrained either to refrain wholly from any further imposition upon such article,

where it had been already rated as high as was proper, or to confine itself to the difference between the existing rate and what the article would reasonably bear. Thus the pre-occupancy of an article by a single State, would tend to arrest or abridge the impositions of the Union on that article. And as it is supposable, that a great variety of articles might be placed in this situation, by dissimilar arrangements of the particular States, it is evident that the aggregate revenue of the country would be likely to be very materially contracted by the plan of separate provisions.

If all the public creditors receive their dues from one source, distributed with an equal hand, their interest will be the same. And, having the same interests, they will unite in the support of the fiscal arrangements of the Government— as these, too, can be made with more convenience where there is no competition. These circumstances combined, will insure to the revenue laws a more ready and more satisfactory execution.

If, on the contrary, there are distinct provisions, there will be distinct interests, drawing different ways. That union and concert of views, among the creditors, which in every Government is of great importance to their security, and to that of public credit, will not only not exist, but will be likely to give place to mutual jealousy and opposition. And from this cause, the operation of the systems which may be adopted, both by the particular States and by the Union, with relation to their respective debts, will be in danger of being counteracted.

There are several reasons, which render it probable that the situation of the State creditors would be worse than that of the creditors of the Union, if there be not a national assumption of the State debts. Of these it will be sufficient to mention two: one, that a principal branch of revenue is exclusively vested in the Union; the other, that a State must always be checked in the imposition of taxes on articles of consumption, from the want of power to extend the same regulation to the other States, and from the tendency of partial duties to injure its industry and commerce.

Should the State creditors stand upon a less eligible footing than the others, it is unnatural to expect they would see with pleasure a provision for them. The influence which their dissatisfaction might have, could not but operate injuriously, both for the creditors and the credit of the United States. Hence it is even the interest of the creditors of the Union, that those of the individual States should be comprehended in a general provision. Any attempt to secure to the former either exclusive or peculiar advantages, would materially hazard their interests. Neither would it be just, that one class of public creditors should be more favored than the other. The objects for which both descriptions of the debt were contracted, are in the main the same. Indeed, a great part of the particular debts of the States has arisen from assumptions by them on account of the Union. And it is most equitable, that there should be the same measure of retribution for all. There is an objection, however, to an assumption of the State debts, which deserves particular notice. It may be supposed, that it would increase the difficulty of an equitable settlement between them and the United States.

The principles of that settlement, whenever they shall be discussed, will require all the moderation and wisdom of the Government. In the opinion of the Secretary, that discussion, till further lights are obtained, would be premature. All, therefore, which he would now think advisable on the point in question, would be, that the amount of the debts assumed and provided for, should be charged to the respective States, to abide an eventual arrangement. This, the United States, as assignees to the creditors, would have an indisputable right to do.

*   *   *

The Secretary, in the views which have directed his pursuit of the subject, has been influenced, in the first place, by the consideration, that his duty, from the very terms of the resolution of the House, obliged him to propose what appeared to him an adequate provision for the support of the public credit, adapted at the same time to the real circumstances of the United States; and, in the next, by the reflection, that measures which will not bear the test of future unbiassed examination, can neither be productive of individual reputation, nor (which is of much greater consequence) public honor or advantage.

Deeply impressed, as the Secretary is, with a full and deliberate conviction that the establishment of the public credit, upon the basis of a satisfactory provision for the public debt, is, under the present circumstances of this country, the true desideratum towards relief from individual and national embarrassments; that, without it, these embarrassments will be likely to press still more severely upon the community; he cannot but indulge an anxious wish, that an effectual plan for that purpose may, during the present session, be the result of the united wisdom of the Legislature.

He is fully convinced that it is of the greatest importance that no further delay should attend the making of the requisite provision: not only because it will give a better impression of the good faith of the country, and will bring earlier relief to the creditors, both which circumstances are of great moment to public credit, but becuse the advantages to the community, from raising stock, as speedily as possible, to its natural value, will be incomparably greater than any that can result from its continuance below that standard. No profit which could be derived from purchases in the market, on account of the Government, to any practicable extent, would be an equivalent for the loss which would be sustained by the purchases of foreigners at a low value. Not to repeat, that governmental purchases, to be honorable, ought to be preceded by a provision. Delay, by disseminating doubt, would sink the price of stock; and, as the temptation to foreign speculations, from the lowness of the price, would be too great to be neglected, millions would probably be lost to the United States.

Alexander Hamilton

REPORT ON MANUFACTURES

Hamilton's report of 1791—a second major segment of the Federalist program—represents one of the most far-sighted state papers ever produced by an American politician. Most Americans in that age were engaged in agriculture and showed a marked reluctance to embark upon manufacturing for two reasons: first, from a conviction that it was economically impossible for the country to challenge the supremacy of European manufactures; secondly, from a belief that manufacturing would have a bad influence, both morally and socially, upon the lives of the people. Running counter to this prevailing prejudice, Hamilton's report stressed the advantages that would accrue to America from manufacturing. The development of industry, he argued, would strengthen rather than weaken agriculture, open opportunities for investors and entrepreneurs, create jobs for workers, and build up America's population by attracting immigrants. Hamilton strongly advocated government aid to industry on the grounds that manufacturing would unite the competing economic interests and benefit the entire nation. Was he being idealistic in trying to harmonize the competing economic interests within the country? If Hamilton was so realistic, why, as a political leader, did he support such an obvious minority position as that of the manufacturers?

THE Secretary of the Treasury, in obedience to the order of the House of Representatives, of the 15th day of January, 1790, has applied his attention, at as early a period as his other duties would permit, to the subject of Manufactures, and particularly to the means of promoting such as will tend to render the United States independent on foreign nations, for military and other essential supplies; and he thereupon respectfully submits the following report:

The expediency of encouraging manufactures in the United States, which was not long since deemed very questionable, appears at this time to be pretty generally admitted. The embarrassments which have obstructed the progress of our external trade, have led to serious reflections on the necessity of enlarging the sphere of our domestic commerce. The restrictive regulations, which, in foreign markets, abridge the vent of the increasing surplus of our agricultural produce, serve to beget an earnest desire, that a more extensive demand for that surplus may be created at home; and the complete success which has rewarded manufacturing enterprise, in some valuable branches, conspiring with the promising symptoms which attend some less mature essays in others, justify a hope, that the obstacles to the growth of this species of industry are less formidable than they were apprehended to be; and that it is not difficult to find, in its further extension, a full indemnification for any external disadvantages, which are or may be experienced, as well as an accession of resources, favorable to national independence and safety.

There still are, nevertheless, respectable patrons of opinions unfriendly to the encouragement of manufactures. The following are, substantially, the arguments by which these opinions are defended.

"In every country (say those who entertain them) agriculture is the most beneficial and productive object of hu-

From John C. Hamilton, ed., *Works of Alexander Hamilton* (New York, 1850–1851), Vol. III, pp. 192–219, 284.

man industry. This position, generally, if not universally true, applies with peculiar emphasis to the United States, on account of their immense tracts of fertile territory, uninhabited and unimproved. Nothing can afford so advantageous an employment for capital and labor, as the conversion of this extensive wilderness into cultivated farms. Nothing, equally with this, can contribute to the population, strength, and real riches of the country.*

"To endeavor, by the extraordinary patronage of government, to accelerate the growth of manufactures, is, in fact, to endeavor, by force and art, to transfer the natural current of industry from a more to a less beneficial channel. Whatever has such a tendency, must necessarily be unwise; indeed, it can hardly ever be wise in a government to attempt to give a direction to the industry of its citizens. This, under the quick-sighted guidance of private interest, will, if left to itself, infallibly find its own way to the most profitable employment; and it is by such employment, that the public prosperity will be most effectually promoted. To leave industry to itself, therefore, is, in almost every case, the soundest as well as the simplest policy.

"This policy is not only recommended to the United States, by considerations which affect all nations; it is, in a manner, dictated to them by the imperious force of a very peculiar situation. The smallness of their population compared with their territory; the constant allurements to emigration from the settled to the unsettled parts of the country: the facility with which the less independent condition of an artisan can be exchanged for the more independent condition of a farmer; these, and similar causes, conspire to produce, and, for a length of time, must continue to occasion, a scarcity of hands for manufacturing occupation, and dearness of labor generally. To these disadvantages for the prosecution

of manufactures, a deficiency of pecuniary capital being added, the prospect of a successful competition with the manufactures of Europe, must be regarded as little less than desperate. Extensive manufactures can only be the offspring of a redundant, at least of a full population. Till the latter shall characterize the situation of this country, 'tis vain to hope for the former.

"If, contrary to the natural course of things, an unseasonable and premature spring can be given to certain fabrics, by heavy duties, prohibitions, bounties, or by other forced expedients, this will only be to sacrifice the interests of the community to those of particular classes. Besides the misdirection of labor, a virtual monopoly will be given to the persons employed on such fabrics; and an enhancement of price, the inevitable consequence of every monopoly, must be defrayed at the expense of the other parts of society. It is far preferable, that those persons should be engaged in the cultivation of the earth, and that we should procure, in exchange for its productions, the commodities with which foreigners are able to supply us in greater perfection, and upon better terms."

This mode of reasoning is founded upon facts and principles which have certainly respectable pretensions. If it had governed the conduct of nations more generally than it has done, there is room to suppose that it might have carried them faster to prosperity and greatness than they have attained by the pursuit of maxims too widely opposite. Most general theories, however, admit of numerous exceptions, and there are few, if any, of the political kind, which do not blend a considerable portion of error with the truths they inculcate.

In order to [have] an accurate judgment how far that which has been just stated ought to be deemed liable to a similar imputation, it is necessary to advert carefully to the considerations which plead in favor of manufactures, and which appear to recommend the special and positive encouragement of them in certain cases, and under certain reasonable limitations.

It ought readily to be conceded that

* In this paragraph as in succeeding paragraphs set off in quotations, Hamilton was apparently paraphrasing Adam Smith's *Wealth of Nations.* See Harold C. Syrett and Jacob E. Cooke, eds., *Papers of Alexander Hamilton* (New York, 1966), Vol. I, 235.

the cultivation of the earth, as the primary and most certain source of national supply; as the immediate and chief source of subsistence to man; as the principal source of those materials which constitute the nutriment of other kinds of labor; as including a state most favorable to the freedom and independence of the human mind—one, perhaps, most conducive to the mutiplication of the human species; has intrinsically a strong claim to pre-eminence over every other kind of industry.

But, that it has a title to any thing like an exclusive predilection, in any country, ought to be admitted with great caution; that it is even more productive than every other branch of industry, requires more evidence than has yet been given in support of the position. That its real interests, precious and important as, without the help of exaggeration, they truly are, will be advanced, rather than injured, by the due encouragement of manufactures, may, it is believed, be satisfactorily demonstrated. And it is also believed, that the expediency of such encouragement, in a general view, may be shown to be recommended by the most cogent and persuasive motives of national policy.

It has been maintained, that agriculture is not only the most productive, but the only productive species of industry. The reality of this suggestion, in either respect, has, however, not been verified by any accurate detail of facts and calculations; and the general arguments which are adduced to prove it, are rather subtile and paradoxical, than solid or convincing.

Those which maintain its exclusive productiveness, are to this effect:

Labor bestowed upon the cultivation of land, produces enough, not only to replace all the necessary expenses incurred in the business, and to maintain the persons who are employed in it, but to afford, together with the ordinary profit on the stock or capital of the farmer, a net surplus or rent for the landlord or proprietor of the soil. But the labor of artificers does nothing more than replace the stock which employs them (or which furnishes materials, tools, and wages), and yield the ordinary profit upon that stock. It yields nothing equivalent to the rent of land; neither does it add any thing to the total value of the whole annual produce of the land and labor of the country. The additional value given to those parts of the produce of land, which are wrought into manufactures, is counterbalanced by the value of those other parts of that produce which are consumed by the manufacturers. It can, therefore, only be by saving or parsimony, not by the positive productiveness of their labor, that the classes of artificers can, in any degree, augment the revenue of the society.

To this it has been answered:

1. "That, inasmuch as it is acknowledged that manufacturing labor re-produces a value equal to that which is expended or consumed in carrying it on, and continues in existence the original stock or capital employed, it ought, on that account, alone, to escape being considered as wholly unproductive. That, though it should be admitted, as alleged, that the consumption of the produce of the soil, by the classes of artificers or manufacturers, is exactly equal to the value added by their labor to the materials upon which it is exerted, yet, it would not thence follow, that it added nothing to the revenue of the society, or to the aggregate value of the annual produce of its land and labor. If the consumption, for any given period, amounted to a given sum, and the increased value of the produce manufactured, in the same period, to a like sum, the total amount of the consumption and production, during that period, would be equal to the two sums, and consequently double the value of the agricultural produce consumed; and, though the increment of value produced by the classes of artificers should, at no time, exceed the value of the produce of the land consumed by them, yet, there would be, at every moment, in consequence of their labor, a greater value of goods in the market than would exist independent of it."

2. "That the position, that artificers can augment the revenue of a society only by parsimony, is true in no other

sense than in one which is equally applicable to husbandmen or cultivators. It may be alike affirmed of all these classes, that the fund acquired by their labor, and destined for their support, is not, in an ordinary way, more than equal to it. And hence, it will follow, that augmentations of the wealth or capital of the community (except in the instances of some extraordinary dexterity or skill), can only proceed, with respect to any of them, from the savings of the more thrifty and parsimonious."

3. "That the annual produce of the land and labor of a country can only be increased in two ways—by some improvement in the productive powers of the useful labor which actually exist within it, or by some increase in the quantity of such labor. That, with regard to the first, the labor of artificers being capable of greater subdivision and simplicity of operation than that of cultivators, it is susceptible, in a proportionably greater degree of improvement in its productive powers, whether to be derived from an accession of skill or from the application of ingenious machinery: in which particular, therefore, the labor employed in the culture of land can pretend to no advantage over that engaged in manufactures. That, with regard to an augmentation of the quantity of useful labor, this, excluding adventitious circumstances, must depend essentially upon an increase of capital, which again must depend upon the savings made out of the revenues of those who furnish or manage that which is at any time employed, whether in agriculture or in manufactures, or in any other way."

But, while the exclusive productiveness of agricultural labor has been thus denied and refuted, the superiority of its productiveness has been conceded without hesitation. As this concession involves a point of considerable magnitude, in relation to maxims of public administration, the grounds on which it rests are worthy of a distinct and particular examination.

One of the arguments made use of in support of the idea, may be pronounced both quaint and superficial. It amounts to this: That, in the productions of the soil, nature co-operates with man; and that the effect of their joint labor must be greater than that of the labor of man alone.

This, however, is far from being a necessary inference. It is very conceivable, that the labor of man alone, laid out upon a work requiring great skill and art to bring it to perfection, may be more productive, in value, than the labor of nature and man combined, when directed towards more simple operations and objects; and when it is recollected to what an extent the agency of nature, in the application of the mechanical powers, is made auxiliary to the prosecution of manufactures, the suggestion which has been noticed loses even the appearance of plausibility.

It might also be observed, with a contrary view, that the labor employed in agriculture, is, in a great measure, periodical and occasional, depending on seasons, and liable to various and long intermissions; while that occupied in many manufactures is constant and regular, extending through the year, embracing, in some instances, night as well as day. It is also probable that there are, among the cultivators of land, more examples of remissness than among artificers. The farmer, from the peculiar fertility of his land, or some other favorable circumstance, may frequently obtain a livelihood, even with a considerable degree of carelessness in the mode of cultivation; but the artisan can with difficulty effect the same object, without exerting himself pretty equally with all those who are engaged in the same pursuit. And if it may likewise be assumed as a fact, that manufactures open a wider field to exertions of ingenuity than agriculture, it would not be a strained conjecture, that the labor employed in the former, being at once more constant, more uniform, and more ingenious, than that which is employed in the latter, will be found, at the same time, more productive.

But it is not meant to lay stress on observations of this nature; they ought only to serve as a counterbalance to those of a similar complexion. Circumstances so vague and general, as well as so abstract, can afford little instruction in a matter of this kind.

Another, and that which seems to be the principal argument offered for the superior productiveness of agricultural labor, turns upon the allegation, that labor employed on manufactures, yields nothing equivalent to the rent of land; or to that net surplus, as it is called, which accrues to the proprietor of the soil.

But this distinction, important as it has been deemed, appears rather verbal than substantial.

It is easily discernible, that what, in the first instance, is divided into two parts, under the denominations of the ordinary profit of the stock of the farmer and rent to the landlord, is, in the second instance, united under the general appellation of the ordinary profit on the stock of the undertaker; and that this formal or verbal distribution constitutes the whole difference in the two cases. It seems to have been overlooked, that the land is itself a stock or capital, advanced or lent by its owner to the occupier or tenant, and that the rent he receives is only the ordinary profit of a certain stock in land, not managed by the proprietor himself, but by another, to whom he lends or lets it, and who, on his part, advances a second capital, to stock and improve the land, upon which he also receives the usual profit. The rent of the landlord and the profit of the farmer are, therefore, nothing more than the ordinary profits of two capitals belonging to two different persons, and united in the cultivation of a farm: as, in the other case, the surplus which arises upon any manufactory, after replacing the expenses of carrying it on, answers to the ordinary profits of one or more capitals engaged in the prosecution of such manufactory. It is said one or more capitals, because, in fact, the same thing which is contemplated in the case of the farm, sometimes happens in that of a manufactory. There is one, who furnishes a part of the capital or lends a part of the money by which it is carried on, and another, who carries it on with the addition of his own capi-

tal. Out of the surplus which remains after defraying expenses, an interest is paid to the money-lender, for the portion of the capital furnished by him, which exactly agrees with the rent paid to the landlord; and the residue of that surplus constitutes the profit of the undertaker or manufacturer, and agrees with what is denominated the ordinary profits on the stock of the farmer. Both together, make the ordinary profits of two capitals employed in a manufactory; as, in the other case, the rent of the landlord and the revenue of the farmer compose the ordinary profits of two capitals employed in the cultivation of a farm.

The rent, therefore, accruing to the proprietor of the land, far from being a criterion of exclusive productiveness, as has been argued, is no criterion even of superior productiveness. The question must still be, whether the surplus, after defraying expenses of a given capital, employed in the purchase and improvement of a piece of land, is greater or less than that of a like capital, employed in the prosecution of a manufactory; or whether the whole value produced from a given capital and a given quantity of labor, employed in one way, be greater or less than the whole value produced from an equal capital and an equal quantity of labor, employed in the other way; or rather, perhaps, whether the business of agriculture, or that of manufactures, will yield the greatest product, according to a compound ratio of the quantity of the capital, and the quantity of labor, which are employed in the one or in the other.

The solution of either of these questions is not easy; it involves numerous and complicated details, depending on an accurate knowledge of the objects to be compared. It is not known that the comparison has ever yet been made upon sufficient data, properly ascertained and analyzed. To be able to make it on the present occasion, with satisfactory precision, would demand more previous inquiry and investigation, than there has been hitherto either leisure or opportunity to accomplish.

Some essays, however, have been

made towards acquiring the requisite information; which have rather served to throw doubt upon, than to confirm the hypothesis under examination. But it ought to be acknowledged, that they have been too little diversified, and are too imperfect to authorize a definitive conclusion either way; leading rather to probable conjecture than to certain deduction. They render it probable that there are various branches of manufactures, in which a given capital will yield a greater total product, and a considerably greater net product, than an equal capital invested in the purchase and improvement of lands; and that there are also some branches, in which both the gross and the net produce will exceed that of agricultural industry, according to a compound ratio of capital and labor. But it is on this last point that there appears to be the greatest room for doubt. It is far less difficult to infer generally, that the net produce of capital engaged in manufacturing enterprises is greater than that of capital engaged in agriculture.

The foregoing suggestions are not designed to inculcate an opinion that manufacturing industry is more productive than that of agriculture. They are intended rather to show that the reverse of this proposition is not ascertained; that the general arguments, which are brought to establish it, are not satisfactory; and consequently, that a supposition of the superior productiveness of tillage ought to be no obstacle to listening to any substantial inducements to the encouragement of manufactures, which may be otherwise perceived to exist, through an apprehension that they may have a tendency to divert labor from a more to a less profitable employment.

It is extremely probable, that, on a full and accurate development of the matter, on the ground of fact and calculation, it would be discovered that there is no material difference between the aggregate productiveness of the one, and of the other kind of industry; and that the propriety of the encouragements, which may, in any case, be proposed to be given to either, ought to be determined upon considerations irrelative to any comparison of that nature.

II. But without contending for the superior productiveness of manufacturing industry, it may conduce to a better judgment of the policy which ought to be pursued respecting its encouragement, to contemplate the subject under some additional aspects, tending not only to confirm the idea that this kind of industry has been improperly represented as unproductive in itself, but to evince, in addition, that the establishment and diffusion of manufactures have the effect of rendering the total mass of useful and productive labor, in a community, greater than it would otherwise be. In prosecuting this discussion, it may be necessary briefly to resume and review some of the topics which have been already touched.

To affirm that the labor of the manufacturer is unproductive, because he consumes as much of the produce of land as he adds value to the raw material which he manufactures, is not better founded, than it would be to affirm that the labor of the farmer, which furnishes materials to the manufacturer, is unproductive, because he consumes an equal value of manufactured articles. Each furnishes a certain portion of the produce of his labor to the other, and each destroys a correspondent portion of the produce of the labor of the other. In the mean time, the maintenance of two citizens, instead of one, is going on; the State has two members instead of one; and they, together, consume twice the value of what is produced from the land.

If, instead of a farmer and artificer, there were a farmer only, he would be under the necessity of devoting a part of his labor to the fabrication of clothing, and other articles, which he would procure of the artificer, in the case of there being such a person; and of course he would be able to devote less labor to the cultivation of his farm, and would draw from it a proportionably less product. The whole quantity of production, in this state of things, in provisions, raw materials, and manufactures, would certainly not exceed in value the amount of what would be produced in provisions and raw materials only, if there were an artificer as well as a farmer.

Again, if there were both an artificer and a farmer, the latter would be left at liberty to pursue exclusively the cultivation of his farm. A greater quantity of provisions and raw materials would, of course, be produced, equal, at least, as has been already observed, to the whole amount of the provisions, raw materials, and manufactures, which would exist on a contrary supposition. The artificer, at the same time, would be going on in the production of manufactured commodities, to an amount sufficient, not only to repay the farmer, in those commodities, for the provisions and materials which were procured from him, but to furnish the artificer himself, with a supply of similar commodities for his own use. Thus, then, there would be two quantities or values in existence, instead of one; and the revenue and consumption would be double, in one case, what it would be in the other.

If, in place of both of these suppositions, there were supposed to be two farmers and no artificer, each of whom applied a part of his labor to the culture of land, and another part to the fabrication of manufactures; in this case, the portion of the labor of both, bestowed upon land, would produce the same quantity of provisions and raw materials only, as would be produced by the entire sum of the labor of one, applied in the same manner; and the portion of the labor of both, bestowed upon manufactures, would produce the same quantity of manufactures only, as would be produced by the entire sum of the labor of one, applied in the same manner. Hence, the produce of the labor of the two farmers would not be greater than the produce of the labor of the farmer and artificer; and hence it results, that the labor of the artificer is as positively productive as that of the farmer, and as positively augments the revenue of the society.

The labor of the artificer replaces to the farmer that portion of his labor with which he provides the materials of exchange with the artificer, and which he would otherwise have been compelled to apply to manufactures; and while the artificer thus enables the farmer to enlarge his stock of agricultural industry, a portion of which he purchases for his own use, he also supplies himself with the manufactured articles, of which he stands in need. He does still more. Besides this equivalent, which he gives for the portion of agricultural labor consumed by him, and this supply of manufactured commodities for his own consumption, he furnishes still a surplus, which compensates for the use of the capital advanced, either by himself or some other person, for carrying on the business. This is the ordinary profit of the stock employed in the manufactory, and is, in every sense, as effective an addition to the income of the society as the rent of land.

The produce of the labor of the artificer, consequently, may be regarded as composed of three parts; one, by which the provisions for his subsistence and the materials for his work, are purchased of the farmer; one, by which he supplies himself with manufactured necessaries; and a third, which constitutes the profit on the stock employed. The two last portions seem to have been overlooked, in the system which represents manufacturing industry as barren and unproductive.

In the course of the preceding illustrations, the products of equal quantities of the labor of the farmer and artificer have been treated as if equal to each other. But this is not to be understood as intending to assert any such precise equality. It is merely a manner of expression, adopted for the sake of simplicity and perspicuity. Whether the value of the produce of the labor of the farmer be somewhat more or less than that of the artificer, is not material to the main scope of the argument, which, hitherto, has only aimed at showing, that the one, as well as the other, occasions a positive augmentation of the total produce and revenue of the society.

It is now proper to proceed a step further, and to enumerate the principal circumstances from which it may be inferred that manufacturing establishments not only occasion a positive augmentation of the produce and revenue of the society, but that they contribute essentially to rendering them greater than they could possibly be, without such establishments. These circumstances are:

1. The division of labor.
2. An extension of the use of machinery.
3. Additional employment to classes of the community not ordinarily engaged in the business.
4. The promoting of emigration from foreign countries.
5. The furnishing greater scope for the diversity of talents and dispositions, which discriminate men from each other.
6. The affording a more ample and various field for enterprise.
7. The creating, in some instances, a new, and securing, in all, a more certain and steady demand for the surplus produce of the soil.

Each of these circumstances has a considerable influence upon the total mass of industrious effort in a community; together, they add to it a degree of energy and effect, which are not easily conceived. Some comments upon each of them, in the order in which they have been stated, may serve to explain their importance.

1. *As to the division of labor.*

It has justly been observed, that there is scarcely any thing of greater moment in the economy of a nation, than the proper division of labor. The separation of occupations, causes each to be carried to a much greater perfection, than it could possibly acquire if they were blended. This arises principally from three circumstances:

1st. The greater skill and dexterity naturally resulting from a constant and undivided application to a single object. It is evident that these properties must increase in proportion to the separation and simplification of objects, and the steadiness of the attention devoted to each; and must be less in proportion to the complication of objects, and the number among which the attention is distracted.

2d. The economy of time, by avoiding the loss of it, incident to a frequent transition from one operation to another of a different nature. This depends on various circumstances; the transition itself, the orderly disposition of the implements, machines, and materials, employed in the operation to be relinquished, the preparatory steps to the commencement of a new one, the interruption of the impulse, which the mind of the workman acquires, from being engaged in a particular operation, the distractions, hesitations, and reluctances, which attend the passage from one kind of business to another.

3d. An extension of the use of machinery. A man occupied on a single object will have it more in his power, and will be more naturally-led to exert his imagination, in devising methods to facilitate and abridge labor, than if he were perplexed by a variety of independent and dissimilar operations. Besides this, the fabrication of machines, in numerous instances, becoming itself a distinct trade, the artist who follows it has all the advantages which have been enumerated, for improvement in his particular art; and, in both ways, the invention and application of machinery are extended.

And from these causes united, the mere separation of the occupation of the cultivator from that of the artificer, has the effect of augmenting the productive powers of labor, and with them, the total mass of the produce or revenue of a country. In this single view of the subject, therefore, the utility of artificers or manufacturers, towards promoting an increase of productive industry, is apparent.

2. *As to an extension of the use of machinery, a point which, though partly anticipated, requires to be placed in one or two additional lights.*

The employment of machinery forms an item of great importance in the general mass of national industry. It is an artificial force brought in aid of the natural force of man; and, to all the purposes of labor, is an increase of hands, an accession of strength, unencumbered too by the expense of maintaining the laborer. May it not, therefore, be fairly inferred, that those occupations which give greatest scope to the use of this auxiliary, contribute most to the general stock of industrious effort, and, in consequence, to the general product of industry?

It shall be taken for granted, and the truth of the position referred to observation, that manufacturing pursuits are susceptible, in a greater degree, of the application of machinery, than those of agriculture. If so, all the difference is lost to a community, which, instead of manufacturing for itself, procures the fabrics requisite to its supply, from other countries. The substitution of foreign for domestic manufactures, is a transfer to foreign nations, of the advantages accruing from the employment of machinery, in the modes in which it is capable of being employed, with most utility and to the greatest extent.

The cotton-mill, invented in England, within the last twenty years, is a signal illustration of the general proposition which has been just advanced. In consequence of it, all the different processes for spinning cotton, are performed by means of machines, which are put in motion by water, and attended chiefly by women and children; and by a smaller number of persons, in the whole, than are requisite in the ordinary mode of spinning. And it is an advantage of great moment, that the operations of this mill continue with convenience, during the night as well as through the day. The prodigious effect of such a machine is easily conceived. To this invention is to be attributed, essentially, the immense progress which has been so suddenly made in Great Britain, in the various fabrics of cotton.

3. *As to the additional employment of classes of the community not originally engaged in the particular business.*

This is not among the least valuable of the means, by which manufacturing institutions contribute to augment the general stock of industry and production. In places where those institutions prevail, besides the persons regularly engaged in them, they afford occasional and extra employment to industrious individuals and families, who are willing to devote the leisure resulting from the intermissions of their ordinary pursuits to collateral labors, as a resource for multiplying their acquisitions or their enjoyments. The husbandman himself experiences a new source of profit and support, from the increased industry of his wife and daughters, invited and stimulated by the demands of the neighboring manufactories.

Besides this advantage of occasional employment to classes having different occupations, there is another, of a nature allied to it, and of a similar tendency. This is the employment of persons who would otherwise be idle, and in many cases, a burthen on the community, either from the bias of temper, habit, infirmity of body, or some other cause, indisposing or disqualifying them for the toils of the country. It is worthy of particular remark, that, in general, women and children are rendered more useful, and the latter more early useful, by manufacturing establishments, than they would otherwise be. Of the number of persons employed in the cotton manufactories of Great Britain, it is computed that four-sevenths, nearly, are women and children; of whom the greatest proportion are children, and many of them of a tender age.

And thus it appears to be one of the attributes of manufactures, and one of no small consequence, to give occasion to the exertion of a greater quantity of industry, even by the same number of persons, where they happen to prevail, than would exist if there were no such establishments.

4. *As to the promoting of emigration from foreign countries.*

Men reluctantly quit one course of occupation and livelihood for another, unless invited to it by very apparent and proximate advantages. Many who would go from one country to another, if they had a prospect of continuing with more benefit the callings to which they have been educated, will often not be tempted to change their situation by the hope of doing better in some other way. Manufacturers, who, listening to the powerful invitations of a better price for their fabrics, or their labor, of greater cheapness of provisions and raw materials, of an exemption from the chief part of the taxes, burthens, and restraints, which they endure in the old world, of greater personal independence and consequence, under the operation of a more equal government, and of what is far more precious than mere religious toleration, a perfect equality of religious privileges, would probably flock from Europe to the United States, to pursue their own trades or professions, if they were once made sensible of the advantages they would enjoy, and were inspired with an assurance of encouragement and employment, will, with difficulty, be induced to transplant themselves, with a view to becoming cultivators of land.

If it be true, then, that it is the interest of the United States to open every possible avenue to emigration from abroad, it affords a weighty argument for the encouragement of manufactures; which, for the reasons just assigned, will have the strongest tendency to multiply the inducements to it.

Here is perceived an important resource, not only for extending the population, and with it the useful and productive labor of the country, but likewise for the prosecution of manufactures, without deducting from the number of hands, which might otherwise be drawn to tillage; and even for the indemnification of agriculture, for such as might happen to be diverted from it. Many, whom manufacturing views would induce to emigrate, would, afterwards, yield to the temptations which the particular situation of this country holds out to agricultural pursuits. And while agriculture would, in other respects, derive many signal and unmingled advantages from the growth of manufactures, it is a problem whether it would gain or lose, as to the article of the number of persons employed in carrying it on.

5. *As to the furnishing greater scope for the diversity of talents and disposi-*tions, which discriminate men from each other.*

This is a much more powerful mean of augmenting the fund of national industry, than may at first sight appear. It is a just observation, that minds of the strongest and most active powers for their proper objects, fall below mediocrity, and labor without effect, if confined to uncongenial pursuits. And it is thence to be inferred, that the results of human exertion may be immensely increased by diversifying its objects. When all the different kinds of industry obtain in a community, each individual can find his proper element, and can call into activity, the whole vigor of his nature. And the community is benefited by the services of its respective members, in the manner in which each can serve it with most effect.

If there be any thing in a remark often to be met with, namely, that there is, in the genius of the people of this country, a peculiar aptitude for mechanic improvements, it would operate as a forcible reason for giving opportunities to the exercise of that species of talent, by the propagation of manufactures.

6. *As to the affording a more ample and various field for enterprise.*

This also is of greater consequence in the general scale of national exertion, than might, perhaps, on a superficial view be supposed, and has effects not altogether dissimilar from those of the circumstance last noticed. To cherish and stimulate the activity of the human mind, by multiplying the objects of enterprise, is not among the least considerable of the expedients by which the wealth of a nation may be promoted. Even things in themselves not positively advantageous, sometimes become so, by their tendency to provoke exertion. Every new scene which is opened to the busy nature of man to rouse and exert itself, is the addition of a new energy to the general stock of effort.

The spirit of enterprise, useful and prolific as it is, must necessarily be contracted or expanded, in proportion to the simplicity or variety of the occupations and productions which are to be found in a society. It must be less in a nation of mere cultivators, than in a nation of cultivators and merchants; less in a nation of cultivators and merchants, than in a nation of cultivators, artificers, and merchants.

7. *As to the creating, in some instances, a new, and securing in all, a more certain and steady demand, for the surplus produce of the soil.*

This is among the most important of the circumstances which have been indicated. It is a principal mean by which the establishment of manufactures contribute to an augmentation of the produce or revenue of a country, and has an immediate and direct relation to the prosperity of agriculture.

It is evident, that the exertions of the husbandman will be steady or fluctuating, vigorous or feeble, in proportion to the steadiness or fluctuation, adequateness or inadequateness of the markets on which he must depend, for the vent of the surplus which may be produced by his labor; and that such surplus, in the ordinary course of things, will be greater or less in the same proportion.

For the purpose of this vent, a domestic market is greatly to be preferred to a foreign one; because it is, in the nature of things, far more to be relied upon.

It is a primary object of the policy of nations, to be able to supply themselves with subsistence from their own soils; and manufacturing nations, as far as circumstances permit, endeavor to procure from the same source, the raw materials necessary for their own fabrics. This disposition, urged by the spirit of monopoly, is sometimes even carried to an injudicious extreme. It seems not always to be recollected, that nations, who have neither mines nor manufactures, can only obtain the manufactured articles of which they stand in need, by an exchange of the products of their soils; and that, if those who can best furnish them with such articles, are unwilling to give a due course to this exchange, they must, of necessity, make every possible effort to manufacture for themselves; the effect of which is, that the manufacturing nations abridge the natural advantages of their situation, through an unwillingness to permit the agricultural countries to enjoy the advantages of theirs, and sacrifice the interests of a mutually beneficial intercourse to the vain project of selling every thing and buying nothing.

But it is also a consequence of the policy which has been noted, that the foreign demand for the products of agricultural countries, is, in a great degree, rather casual and occasional, than certain or constant. To what extent injurious interruptions of the demand for some of the staple commodities of the United States may have been experienced from that cause, must be referred to the judgment of those who are engaged in carrying on the commerce of the country; but, it may be safely affirmed, that such interruptions are, at times, very inconveniently felt, and that cases not unfrequently occur, in which markets are so confined and restricted, as to render the demand very unequal to the supply.

Independently, likewise, of the artificial impediments which are created by the policy in question, there are natural causes tending to render the external demand for the surplus of agricultural nations a precarious reliance. The differences of seasons in the countries which are the consumers, make immense differences in the produce of their own soils, in different years; and consequently in the degrees of their necessity for foreign supply. Plentiful harvest with them, especially if similar ones occur at the same time in the countries which are the furnishers, occasion, of course, a glut in the markets of the latter.

Considering how fast, and how much the progress of new settlements, in the United States, must increase the surplus produce of the soil, and weighing seriously the tendency of the system which prevails among most of the commercial nations of Europe; whatever dependence may be placed on the force of natural circumstances to counteract the effects of an artificial policy, there appear strong reasons to regard the foreign demand for that surplus, as too uncertain a reliance, and to desire a substitute for it in an extensive domestic market.

To secure such a market there is no other expedient than to promote manufacturing establishments. Manufacturers who constitute the most numerous class, after the cultivators of land, are for that reason the principal consumers of the surplus of their labor.

This idea of an extensive domestic market for the surplus produce of the soil, is of the first consequence. It is, of all things, that which most effectually conduces to a flourishing state of agriculture. If the effect of manufactories should be to detach a portion of the hands which would otherwise be engaged in tillage, it might possibly cause a smaller quantity of lands to be under cultivation; but, by their tendency to procure a more certain demand for the surplus produce of the soil, they would, at the same time, cause the lands which were in cultivation to be better improved and more productive. And while, by their influence, the condition of each individual farmer would be meliorated, the total mass of agricultural production would probably be increased. For this must evidently depend as much upon the degree of improvement, if not more, than upon the number of acres under culture.

It merits particular observation, that the multiplication of manufactories not only furnishes a market for those articles which have been accustomed to be produced in abundance in a country; but it likewise creates a demand for such as were either unknown, or produced in inconsiderable quantities. The bowels, as well as the surface of the earth, are ransacked for articles which were before neglected. Animals, plants, and minerals, acquire an utility and value which were before unexplored.

The foregoing considerations seem sufficient to establish, as general propositions, that it is the interest of nations to diversify the industrious pursuits of the individuals who compose them. That the establishment of manufactures is calculated not only to increase the general stock of useful and productive labor, but even to improve the state of

agriculture in particular; certainly to advance the interests of those who are engaged in it. There are other views that will be hereafter taken of the subject, which it is conceived will serve to confirm these inferences.

III. Previously to a further discussion of the objections to the encouragement of manufactures, which have been stated, it will be of use to see what can be said in reference to the particular situation of the United States, against the conclusions appearing to result from what has been already offered.

It may be observed, and the idea is of no inconsiderable weight, that, however true it might be, that a State which, possessing large tracts of vacant and fertile territory, was, at the same time, secluded from foreign commerce, would find its interest and the interest of agriculture, in diverting a part of its population from tillage to manufactures; yet it will not follow, that the same is true of a State which, having such vacant and fertile territory, has, at the same time, ample opportunity of procuring from abroad, on good terms, all the fabrics of which it stands in need, for the supply of its inhabitants. The power of doing this, at least secures the great advantage of a division of labor, leaving the farmer free to pursue, exclusively, the culture of his land, and enabling him to procure with its products the manufactured supplies requisite either to his wants or to his enjoyments. And though it should be true that, in settled countries, the diversification of industry is conducive to an increase in the productive powers of labor, and to an augmentation of revenue and capital; yet it is scarcely conceivable that there can be any thing of so solid and permanent advantage to an uncultivated and unpeopled country, as to convert its wastes into cultivated and inhabited districts. If the revenue, in the mean time, should be less, the capital, in the event, must be greater.

To these observations, the following appears to be a satisfactory answer:

1st. If the system of perfect liberty to industry and commerce were the pre-

vailing system of nations, the arguments
which dissuade a country, in the predic-
ament of the United States, from the
zealous pursuit of manufactures, would
doubtless have great force. It will not
be affirmed that they might not be permitted, with few exceptions, to serve as
a rule of national conduct. In such a state
of things, each country would have the
full benefit of its peculiar advantages to
compensate for its deficiencies or disadvantages. If one nation were in a condition to supply manufactured articles,
on better terms than another, that other
might find an abundant indemnification
in a superior capacity to furnish the produce of the soil. And a free exchange,
mutually beneficial, of the commodities
which each was able to supply, on the
best terms, might be carried on between
them, supporting, in full vigor, the industry of each. And though the circumstances which have been mentioned,
and others which will be unfolded hereafter, render it probable that nations,
merely agricultural, would not enjoy the
same degree of opulence, in proportion
to their numbers, as those which united
manufactures with agriculture; yet the
progressive improvement of the lands of
the former might, in the end, atone for
an inferior degree of opulence in the
mean time; and in a case in which opposite considerations are pretty equally
balanced, the option ought, perhaps, always to be in favor of leaving industry
to its own direction.

But the system which has been mentioned, is far from characterizing the
general policy of nations. The prevalent one has been regulated by an opposite spirit. The consequence of it is, that
the United States are, to a certain extent,
in the situation of a country precluded
from foreign commerce. They can, indeed, without difficulty, obtain from
abroad the manufactured supplies of
which they are in want; but they experience numerous and very injurious
impediments to the emission and vent
of their own commodities. Nor is this
the case in reference to a single foreign
nation only. The regulations of several
countries, with which we have the most
extensive intercourse, throw serious obstructions in the way of the principal
staples of the United States.

In such a position of things, the
United States cannot exchange with Europe on equal terms; and the want of rec-
iprocity would render them the victim
of a system which should induce them
to confine their views to agriculture,
and refrain from manufactures. A constant and increasing necessity, on their
part, for the commodities of Europe,
and only a partial and occasional demand for their own, in return, could not
but expose them to a state of impover-
ishment, compared with the opulence
to which their political and natural advantages authorize them to aspire.

Remarks of this kind are not made in
the spirit of complaint. It is for the nations whose regulations are alluded to,
to judge for themselves, whether, by aim-
ing at too much, they do not lose more
than they gain. It is for the United States
to consider by what means they can
render themselves least dependent on
the combinations, right or wrong, of foreign policy.

It is no small consolation, that, already, the measures which have embar-
rassed our trade, have accelerated internal improvements, which, upon the
whole, have bettered our affairs. To diversify and extend these improvements
is the surest and safest method of indemnifying ourselves for any inconveniences which those or similar measures
have a tendency to beget. If Europe will
not take from us the products of our
soil, upon terms consistent with our interest, the natural remedy is to contract,
as fast as possible, our wants of her.

2d. The conversion of their waste into
cultivated lands, is certainly a point of
great moment, in the political calculations of the United States. But the degree
in which this may possibly be retarded,
by the encouragement of manufactories,
does not appear to countervail the powerful inducements to afford that encouragement.

An observation made in another place,
is of a nature to have great influence
upon this question. If it cannot be de-

nied, that the interests, even of agriculture, may be advanced more by having such of the lands of a State as are occupied, under good cultivation, than by having a greater quantity occupied under a much inferior cultivation; and if manufactories, for the reasons assigned, must be admitted to have a tendency to promote a more steady and vigorous cultivation of the lands occupied, than would happen without them, it will follow that they are capable of indemnifying a country for a diminution of the progress of new settlements; and may serve to increase both the capital value, and the income of its lands, even though they should abridge the number of acres under tillage.

But it does by no means follow, that the progress of new settlements would be retarded by the extension of manufactures. The desire of being an independent proprietor of land, is founded on such strong principles in the human breast, that, where the opportunity of becoming so is as great as it is in the United States, the proportion will be small of those whose situations would otherwise lead to it, who would be diverted from it towards manufactures. And it is highly probable, as already intimated, that the accessions of foreigners, who, originally drawn over by manufacturing views, would afterwards abandon them for agricultural, would be more than an equivalent for those of our own citizens who might happen to be detached from them.

The remaining objections to a particular encouragement of manufactures in the United States, now require to be examined.

One of these turns on the proposition, that industry, if left to itself, will naturally find its way to the most useful and profitable employment. Whence it is inferred, that manufactures, without the aid of government, will grow up as soon and as fast as the natural state of things and the interest of the community may require.

Against the solidity of this hypothesis, in the full latitude of the terms, very cogent reasons may be offered. These have relation to the strong influence of habit and the spirit of imitation; the fear of want of success in untried enterprises; the intrinsic difficulties incident to first essays toward a competition with those who have previously attained to perfection in the business to be attempted; the bounties, premiums, and other artificial encouragements, with which foreign nations second the exertions of their own citizens, in the branches in which they are to be rivalled.

Experience teaches, that men are often so much governed by what they are accustomed to see and practise, that the simplest and most obvious improvements, in the most ordinary occupations, are adopted with hesitation, reluctance, and by slow gradations. The spontaneous transition to new pursuits, in a community long habituated to different ones, may be expected to be attended with proportionably greater difficulty. When former occupations ceased to yield a profit adequate to the subsistence of their followers; or when there was an absolute deficiency of employment in them, owing to the superabundance of hands, changes would ensue; but these changes would be likely to be more tardy than might consist with the interest either of individuals or of the society. In many cases they would not happen, while a bare support could be insured by an adherence to ancient courses, though a resort to a more profitable employment might be practicable. To produce the desirable changes as early as may be expedient, may therefore require the incitement and patronage of government.

The apprehension of failing in new attempts, is, perhaps, a more serious impediment. There are dispositions apt to be attracted by the mere novelty of an undertaking; but these are not always those best calculated to give it success. To this it is of importance that the confidence of cautious, sagacious capitalists, both citizens and foreigners, should be excited. And to inspire this description of persons with confidence, it is essential that they should be made to see in any project which is new—and for that reason alone, if for no other, precarious

—the prospect of such a degree of countenance and support from government, as may be capable of overcoming the obstacles inseparable from first experiments.

The superiority antecedently enjoyed by nations who have preoccupied and perfected a branch of industry, constitutes a more formidable obstacle than either of those which have been mentioned, to the introduction of the same branch into a country in which it did not before exist. To maintain, between the recent establishments of one country, and the long matured establishments of another country, a competition upon equal terms, both as to quality and price, is, in most cases, impracticable. The disparity, in the one, or in the other, or in both, must necessarily be so considerable, as to forbid a successful rivalship, without the extraordinary aid and protection of government.

But the greatest obstacle of all to the successful prosecution of a new branch of industry in a country in which it was before unknown, consists, as far as the instances apply, in the bounties, premiums, and other aids, which are granted in a variety of cases, by the nations in which the establishments to be imitated are previously introduced. It is well known (and particular examples, in the course of this report, will be cited) that certain nations grant bounties on the exportation of particular commodities, to enable their own workmen to undersell and supplant all competitors in the countries to which those commodities are sent. Hence the undertakers of a new manufacture have to contend, not only with the natural disadvantages of a new undertaking, but with the gratuities and remunerations which other governments bestow. To be enabled to contend with success, it is evident that the interference and aid of their own governments are indispensable.

Combinations by those engaged in a particular branch of business, in one country, to frustrate the first efforts to introduce it into another, by temporary sacrifices, recompensed, perhaps, by extraordinary indemnifications of the government of such country, are believed to have existed, and are not to be regarded as destitute of probability. The existence or assurance of aid from the government of the country in which the business is to be introduced, may be essential to fortify adventurers against the dread of such combinations; to defeat their effects, if formed; and to prevent their being formed, by demonstrating that they must in the end prove fruitless.

Whatever room there may be for an expectation, that the industry of a people, under the direction of private interest, will, upon equal terms, find out the most beneficial employment for itself, there is none for a reliance, that it will struggle against the force of unequal terms, or will, of itself, surmount all the adventitious barriers to a successful competition, which may have been erected, either by the advantages naturally acquired from practice, and previous possession of the ground, or by those which may have sprung from positive regulations and an artificial policy. This general reflection might alone suffice as an answer to the objection under examination, exclusively of the weighty considerations which have been particularly urged.

The objections to the pursuit of manufactures in the United States, which next present themselves to discussion, represent an impracticability of success, arising from three causes: scarcity of hands, dearness of labor, want of capital.

The two first circumstances are, to a certain extent, real; and, within due limits, ought to be admitted as obstacles to the success of manufacturing enterprise in the United States. But there are various considerations which lessen their force, and tend to afford an assurance, that they are not sufficient to prevent the advantageous prosecution of many very useful and extensive manufactories.

*　　*　　*

In countries where there is great private wealth, much may be effected by the voluntary contributions of patriotic individuals; but in a community situated like that of the United States, the public purse must supply the deficiency of private resource. In what can it be so useful, as in prompting and improving the efforts of industry?

George Washington

FAREWELL ADDRESS

Washington believed, in theory, that the president should be above factional or party politics. In practice, however, the increasing bitterness of the power struggle between the Federalists and Republicans forced him to recognize that parties were an integral part of the nation's political system. The Farewell Address, written with Hamilton's help, was regarded by some as a partisan document designed to ensure John Adams' victory over Thomas Jefferson in the 1796 election. Could Washington's warning about the "baneful effects" of parties have been directed against the Republicans only? Did Washington condemn party strife solely because he felt that partisan politics were contrary to the country's best interests?

FRIENDS, and Fellow-Citizens: The period for a new election of a Citizen, to Administer the Executive government of the United States, being not far distant, and the time actually arrived, when your thoughts must be employed in designating the person, who is to be cloathed with that important trust, it appears to me proper, especially as it may conduce to a more distinct expression of the public voice, that I should now apprise you of the resolution I have formed, to decline being considered among the number of those, out of whom a choice is to be made.

I beg you, at the same time, to do me the justice to be assured, that this resolution has not been taken, without a strict regard to all the considerations appertaining to the relation, which binds a dutiful citizen to his country, and that, in withdrawing the tender of service which silence in my situation might imply, I am influenced by no diminution of zeal for your future interest, no deficiency of grateful respect for your past kindness; but am supported by a full conviction that the step is compatible with both.

The acceptance of, and continuance hitherto in, the office to which your Suffrages have twice called me, have been a uniform sacrifice of inclination to the opinion of duty, and to a deference for what appeared to be your desire. I constantly hoped, that it would have been much ealier in my power, consistently with motives, which I was not at liberty to disregard, to return to that retirement, from which I have been reluctantly drawn. The strength of my inclination to do this, previous to the last Election, had even led to the preparation of an address to declare it to you; but mature reflection on the then perplexed and critical posture of our Affairs with foreign Nations, and the unanimous advice of persons entitled to my confidence, impelled me to abandon the idea.

I rejoice, that the state of your concerns, external as well as internal, no longer renders the pursuit of inclination incompatible with the sentiment of duty, or propriety; and am persuaded whatever partiality may be retained for my services, that in the present circumstances of our country, you will not disapprove my determination to retire.

The impressions, with which I first undertook the arduous trust, were explained on the proper occasion. In the discharge of this trust, I will only say, that I have, with good intentions, contributed towards the Organization and Administration of the government, the best exertions of which a very fallible judgment was capable. Not unconscious, in the outset, of the inferiority of my

From John C. Fitzpatrick, ed., *The Writings of George Washington* . . . (38 Vols., Washington, G.P.O., 1940) Vol. 35, pp. 214–238.

qualifications, experience in my own eyes, perhaps still more in the eyes of others, has strengthened the motives to diffidence of myself; and every day the encreasing weight of years admonishes me more and more, that the shade of retirement is as necessary to me as it will be welcome. Satisfied that if any circumstances have given peculiar value to my services, they were temporary, I have the consolation to believe, that while choice and prudence invite me to quit the political scene, patriotism does not forbid it.

In looking forward to the moment, which is intended to terminate the career of my public life, my feelings do not permit me to suspend the deep acknowledgment of that debt of gratitude wch. I owe to my beloved country, for the many honors it has conferred upon me; still more for the stedfast confidence with which it has supported me; and for the opportunities I have thence enjoyed of manifesting my inviolable attachment, by services faithful and persevering, though in usefulness unequal to my zeal. If benefits have resulted to our country from these services, let it always be remembered to your praise, and as an instructive example in our annals, that, under circumstances in which the Passions agitated in every direction were liable to mislead, amidst appearances sometimes dubious, viscissitudes of fortune often discouraging, in situations in which not unfrequently want of Success has countenanced the spirit of criticism, the constancy of your support was the essential prop of the efforts, and a guarantee of the plans by which they were effected. Profoundly penetrated with this idea, I shall carry it with me to my grave, as a strong incitement to unceasing vows that Heaven may continue to you the choicest tokens of its beneficence; that your Union and brotherly affection may be perpetual; that the free constitution, which is the work of your hands, may be sacredly maintained; that its Administration in every department may be stamped with wisdom and Virtue; that, in fine, the happiness of the people of these States, under the auspices of liberty, may be made complete, by so careful a preservation and so prudent a use of this blessing as will acquire to them the glory of recommending it to the applause, the affection, and adoption of every nation which is yet a stranger to it.

Here, perhaps, I ought to stop. But a solicitude for your welfare, which cannot end but with my life, and the apprehension of danger, natural to that solicitude, urge me on an occasion like the present, to offer to your solemn contemplation, and to recommend to your frequent review, some sentiments; which are the result of much reflection, of no inconsiderable observation, and which appear to me all important to the permanency of your felicity as a People. These will be offered to you with the more freedom, as you can only see in them the distinterested warnings of a parting friend, who can possibly have no personal motive to biass his counsel. Nor can I forget, as an encouragement to it, your endulgent reception of my sentiments on a former and not dissimilar occasion.

Interwoven as is the love of liberty with every ligament of your hearts, no recommendation of mine is necessary to fortify or confirm the attachment.

The Unity of Government which constitutes you one people is also now dear to you. It is justly so; for it is a main Pillar in the Edifice of your real independence, the support of your tranquility at home; your peace abroad; of your safety; of your prosperity; of that very Liberty which you so highly prize. But as it is easy to foresee, that from different causes and from different quarters, much pains will be taken, many artifices employed, to weaken in your minds the conviction of this truth; as this is the point in your political fortress against which the batteries of internal and external enemies will be most constantly and actively (though often covertly and insidiously) directed, it is of infinite moment, that you should properly estimate the immense value of your national Union to your collective and individual happiness; that you should cherish a cordial, habitual and immoveable attachment to it; accustoming yourselves to think and speak of it as of the Palladium of your political safety and prosperity; watching for its preservation with jealous anxiety; discountenancing whatever may suggest even a suspicion that it can in any event be abandoned, and indignantly frowning upon the first dawning of every attempt to alienate any portion of our Country from the rest, or to enfeeble the sacred ties which now link together the various parts.

For this you have every inducement of sympathy and interest. Citizens by birth or choice, of a common country, that country has a right to concentrate your affections. The name of American, which belongs to you, in your national capacity, must always exalt the just pride of Patriotism, more than any appellation derived from local discriminations. With slight shades of difference, you have the same Religeon, Manners, Habits and political Principles. You have in a common cause fought and triumphed together. The independence and liberty you possess are the work of joint councils, and joint efforts; of common dangers, sufferings and successes.

But these considerations, however powerfully they address themselves to your sensibility are greatly outweighed by those which apply more immediately to your Interest. Here every portion of our country finds the most commanding motives for carefully guarding and preserving the Union of the whole.

The *North*, in an unrestrained intercourse with the *South*, protected by the equal Laws of a common government, finds in the productions of the latter, great additional resources of Maritime and commercial enterprise and precious materials of manufacturing industry. The *South* in the same Intercourse, benefitting by the Agency of the *North*, sees its agriculture grow and its commerce expand. Turning partly into its own channels the seamen of the *North*, it finds its particular navigation envigorated; and while it contributes, in different ways, to nourish and increase the general mass of the National navigation, it looks forward to the protection of a Maritime strength, to which itself is

unequally adapted. The *East*, in a like intercourse with the *West*, already finds, and in the progressive improvement of interior communications, by land and water, will more and more find a valuable vent for the commodities which it brings from abroad, or manufactures at home. The *West* derives from the *East* supplies requisite to its growth and comfort, and what is perhaps of still greater consequence, it must of necessity owe the *secure* enjoyment of indispensable *outlets* for its own productions to the weight, influence, and the future Maritime strength of the Atlantic side of the Union, directed by an indissoluble community of Interest as *one Nation*. Any other tenure by which the *West* can hold this essential advantage, whether derived from its own separate strength, or from an apostate and unnatural connection with any foreign Power, must be intrinsically precarious.

While then every part of our country thus feels an immediate and particular Interest in Union, all the parts combined cannot fail to find in the united mass of means and efforts greater strength, greater resource, proportionably greater security from external danger, a less frequent interruption of their Peace by foreign Nations; and, what is of inestimable value! they must derive from Union an exemption from those broils and Wars between themselves, which so frequently afflict neighbouring countries, not tied together by the same government; which their own rivalships alone would be sufficient to produce, but which opposite foreign alliances, attachments and intrigues would stimulate and imbitter. Hence likewise they will avoid the necessity of those overgrown Military establishments, which under any form of Government are inauspicious to liberty, and which are to be regarded as particularly hostile to Republican Liberty: In this sense it is, that your Union ought to be considered as a main prop of your liberty, and that the love of the one ought to endear to you the preservation of the other.

These considerations speak a persuasive language to every reflecting and virtuous mind, and exhibit the continuance of the UNION as a primary object of Patriotic desire. Is there a doubt, whether a common government can embrace so large a sphere? Let experience solve it. To listen to mere speculation in such a case were criminal. We are authorized to hope that a proper organization of the whole, with the auxiliary agency of governments for the respective Sub divisions, will afford a happy issue to the experiment. 'Tis well worth a fair and full experiment. With such powerful and obvious motives to Union, affecting all parts of our country, while experience shall not have demonstrated its impracticability, there will always be reason, to distrust the patriotism of those, who in any quarter may endeavor to weaken its bands.

In contemplating the causes wch. may disturb our Union, it occurs as matter of serious concern, that any ground should have been furnished for characterizing parties by *Geographical* discriminations: *Northern* and *Southern; Atlantic* and *Western;* whence designing men may endeavour to excite a belief that there is a real difference of local interests and views. One of the expedients of Party to acquire influence, within particular districts, is to misrepresent the opinions and aims of other Districts. You cannot shield yourselves too much against the jealousies and heart burnings which spring from these misrepresentations. They tend to render Alien to each other those who ought to be bound together by fraternal affection. The Inhabitants of our Western country have lately had a useful lesson on this head. They have seen, in the Negociation by the Executive, and in the unanimous ratification by the Senate, of the Treaty with Spain, and in the universal satisfaction at that event, throughout the United States, a decisive proof how unfounded were the suspicions propagated among them of a policy in the General Government and in the Atlantic States unfriendly to their Interests in regard to the MISSISSIPPI. They have been witnesses to the formation of two Treaties, that with G: Britain and that with Spain, which secure to them every thing they could desire, in respect to our Foreign

relations, towards confirming their prosperity. Will it not be their wisdom to rely for the preservation of [*sic*] these advantages on the UNION by wch. they were procured? Will they not henceforth be deaf to those advisers, if such there are, who would sever them from their Brethren and connect them with Aliens?

To the efficacy and permanency of Your Union, a Government for the whole is indispensable. No Alliances however strict between the parts can be an adequate substitute. They must inevitably experience the infractions and interruptions which all Alliances in all times have experienced. Sensible of this momentous truth, you have improved upon your first essay, by the adoption of a Constitution of Government, better calculated than your former for an intimate Union, and for the efficacious management of your common concerns. This government, the offspring of our own choice uninfluenced and unawed, adopted upon full investigation and mature deliberation, completely free in its principles, in the distribution of its powers, uniting security with energy, and containing within itself a provision for its own amendment, has a just claim to your confidence and your support. Respect for its authority, compliance with its Laws, acquiescence in its measures, are duties enjoined by the fundamental maxims of true Liberty. The basis of our political systems is the right of the people to make and to alter their Constitutions of Government. But the Constitution which at any time exists, 'till changed by an explicit and authentic act of the whole People, is sacredly obligatory upon all. The very idea of the power and the right of the People to establish Government presupposes the duty of every Individual to obey the established Government.

All obstructions to the execution of the Laws, all combinations and Associations, under whatever plausible character, with the real design to direct, controul, counteract, or awe the regular deliberation and action of the Constituted authorities are distructive of this fundamental principle and of fatal tendency. They serve to organize faction, to give it an artificial and extraordinary force; to put in the place of the delegated will of the Nation, the will of a party; often a small but artful and enterprizing minority of the Community; and, according to the alternate triumphs of different parties, to make the public administration the Mirror of the ill concerted and incongruous projects of faction, rather than the organ of consistent and wholesome plans digested by common councils and modefied by mutual interests. However combinations or Associations of the above description may now and then answer popular ends, they are likely, in the course of time and things, to become potent engines, by which cunning, ambitious and unprincipled men will be enabled to subvert the Power of the People, and to usurp for themselves the reins of Government; destroying afterwards the very engines which have lifted them to unjust dominion.

Towards the preservation of your Government and the permanency of your present happy state, it is requisite, not only that you steadily discountenance irregular oppositions to its acknowledged authority, but also that you resist with care the spirit of innovation upon its principles however specious the pretexts. One method of assault may be to effect, in the forms of the Constitution, alterations which will impair the energy of the system, and thus to undermine what cannot be directly overthrown. In all the changes to which you may be invited, remember that time and habit are at least as necessary to fix the true character of Governments, as of other human institutions; that experience is the surest standard, by which to test the real tendency of the existing Constitution of a country; that facility in changes upon the credit of mere hypotheses and opinion exposes to perpetual change, from the endless variety of hypotheses and opinion: and remember, especially, that for the efficient management of your common interests, in a country so extensive as ours, a Government of as much vigour as is consistent with the perfect security of Liberty is indispensable. Liberty itself will find in such a Government, with powers properly distributed and adjusted, its surest Guardian. It is indeed little else than a name, where the Government is too feeble to withstand the enterprises of faction, to confine each member of the Society within the limits prescribed by the laws and to maintain all in the secure and tranquil enjoyment of the rights of person and property.

I have already intimated to you the danger of Parties in the State, with particular reference to the founding of them on Geographical discriminations. Let me now take a more comprehensive view, and warn you in the most solemn manner against the baneful effects of the Spirit of Party, generally.

This spirit, unfortunately, is inseparable from our nature, having its root in the strongest passions of the human Mind. It exists under different shapes in all Governments, more or less stifled, controuled, or repressed; but, in those of the popular form it is seen in its greatest rankness and is truly their worst enemy.

The alternate domination of one faction over another, sharpened by the spirit of revenge natural to party dissention, which in different ages and countries has perpetrated the most horrid enormities, is itself a frightful despotism. But this leads at length to a more formal and permanent despotism. The disorders and miseries, which result, gradually incline the minds of men to seek security and repose in the absolute power of an Individual: and sooner or later the chief of some prevailing faction more able or more fortunate than his competitors, turns this disposition to the purposes of his own elevation, on the ruins of Public Liberty.

Without looking forward to an extremity of this kind (which nevertheless ought not to be entirely out of sight) the common and continual mischiefs of the spirit of Party are sufficient to make it the interest and the duty of a wise People to discourage and restrain it.

It serves always to distract the Public Councils and enfeeble the Public administration. It agitates the Community with ill founded jealousies and false alarms, kindles the animosity of one part against another, foments occasionally riot and insurrection. It opens the door to foreign influence and corruption, which find a facilitated access to the government itself through the channels of party passions. Thus the policy and and [*sic*] the will of one country, are subjected to the policy and will of another.

There is an opinion that parties in free countries are useful checks upon the Administration of the Government and serve to keep alive the spirit of Liberty. This within certain limits is probably true, and in Governments of a Monarchical cast Patriotism may look with endulgence, if not with favour, upon the spirit of party. But in those of the popular character, in Governments purely elective, it is a spirit not to be encouraged. From their natural tendency, it is certain there will always be enough of that spirit for every salutary purpose. And there being constant danger of excess, the effort ought to be, by force of public opinion, to mitigate and assuage it. A fire not to be quenched; it demands a uniform vigilance to prevent its bursting into a flame, lest instead of warming it should consume.

It is important, likewise, that the habits of thinking in a free Country should inspire caution in those entrusted with its administration, to confine themselves within their respective Constitutional spheres; avoiding in the exercise of the Powers of one department to encroach upon another. The spirit of encroachment tends to consolidate the powers of all the departments in one, and thus to create, whatever the form of government, a real despotism. A just estimate of that love of power, and proneness to abuse it, which predominates in the human heart is sufficient to satisfy us of the truth of this position. The necessity of reciprocal checks in the exercise of political power; by dividing and distributing it into different depositories, and constituting each the Guardian of the Public Weal against invasions by the others, has been evinced by experiments ancient and modern; some of them in our country and under our own eyes. To preserve them must be as necessary

as to institute them. If in the opinion of the People, the distribution or modification of the Constitutional powers be in any particular wrong, let it be corrected by an amendment in the way which the Constitution designates. But let there be no change by usurpation; for though this, in one instance, may be the instrument of good, it is the customary weapon by which free governments are destroyed. The precedent must always greatly overbalance in permanent evil any partial or transient benefit which the use can at any time yield.

Of all the dispositions and habits which lead to political prosperity, Religion and morality are indispensable supports. In vain would that man claim the tribute of Patriotism, who should labour to subvert these great Pillars of human happiness, these firmest props of the duties of Men and citizens. The mere Politician, equally with the pious man ought to respect and to cherish them. A volume could not trace all their connections with private and public felicity. Let it simply be asked where is the security for property, for reputation, for life, if the sense of religious obligation *desert* the oaths, which are the instruments of investigation in Courts of Justice? And let us with caution indulge the supposition, that morality can be maintained without religion. Whatever may be conceded to the influence of refined education on minds of peculiar structure, reason and experience both forbid us to expect that National morality can prevail in exclusion of religious principle.

'Tis substantially true, that virtue or morality is a necessary spring of popular government. The rule indeed extends with more or less force to every species of free Government. Who that is a sincere friend to it, can look with indifference upon attempts to shake the foundation of the fabric.

Promote then as an object of primary importance, Institutions for the general diffusion of knowledge. In proportion as the structure of a government gives force to public opinion, it is essential that public opinion should be enlightened.

As a very important source of strength

and security, cherish public credit. One method of preserving it is to use it as sparingly as possible: avoiding occasions of expence by cultivating peace, but remembering also that timely disbursements to prepare for danger frequently prevent much greater disbursements to repel it; avoiding likewise the accumulation of debt, not only by shunning occasions of expence, but by vigorous exertions in time of Peace to discharge the Debts which unavoidable wars may have occasioned, not ungenerously throwing upon posterity the burthen which we ourselves ought to bear. The execution of these maxims belongs to your Representatives, but it is necessary that public opinion should cooperate. To facilitate to them the performance of their duty, it is essential that you should practically bear in mind, that towards the payment of debts there must be Revenue; that to have Revenue there must be taxes; that no taxes can be devised which are not more or less inconvenient and unpleasant; that the intrinsic embarrassment inseperable from the selection of the proper objects (which is always a choice of difficulties) ought to be a decisive motive for a candid construction of the Conduct of the Government in making it, and for a spirit of acquiescence in the measures for obtaining Revenue which the public exigencies may at any time dictate.

Observe good faith and justice towds. all Nations. Cultivate peace and harmony with all. Religion and morality enjoin this conduct; and can it be that good policy does not equally enjoin it? It will be worthy of a free, enlightened, and, at no distant period, a great Nation, to give to mankind the magnanimous and too novel example of a People always guided by an exalted justice and benevolence. Who can doubt that in the course of time and things the fruits of such a plan would richly repay any temporary advantages wch. might be lost by a steady adherence to it? Can it be, that Providence has not connected the permanent felicity of a Nation with its virtue? The experiment, at least is recommended by every sentiment which ennobles human Nature. Alas! is it rendered impossible by its vices?

In the execution of such a plan nothing is more essential than that permanent, inveterate antipathies against particular Nations and passionate attachments for others should be excluded; and that in place of them just and amicable feelings towards all should be cultivated. The Nation, which indulges towards another an habitual hatred, or an habitual fondness, is in some degree a slave. It is a slave to its animosity or to its affection, either of which is sufficient to lead it astray from its duty and its interest. Antipathy in one Nation against another, disposes each more readily to offer insult and injury, to lay hold of slight causes of umbrage, and to be haughty and intractable, when accidental or trifling occasions of dispute occur. Hence frequent collisions, obstinate envenomed and bloody contests. The Nation, prompted by illwill and resentment sometimes impels to War the Government, contrary to the best calculations of policy. The Government sometimes participates in the national propensity, and adopts through passion what reason would reject; at other times, it makes the animosity of the Nation subservient to projects of hostility instigated by pride, ambition and other sinister and pernicious motives. The peace often, sometimes perhaps the Liberty, of Nations has been the victim.

So likewise, a passionate attachment of one Nation for another produces a variety of evils. Sympathy for the favourite nation, facilitating the illusion of an imaginary common interest, in cases where no real common interest exists, and infusing into one the enmities of the other, betrays the former into a participation in the quarrels and Wars of the latter, without adequate inducement or justification: It leads also to concessions to the favourite Nation of priviledges denied to others, which is apt doubly to injure the Nation making the concessions; by unnecessarily parting with what ought to have been retained; and by exciting jealousy, ill will, and a disposition to retaliate, in the parties from whom eql. priviledges are withheld: And it gives to ambitious, corrupted, or deluded citizens (who devote themselves to the favourite Nation) facility to betray, or sacrifice the interests of their own country, without odium, sometimes even with popularity; gilding with the appearances of a virtuous sense of obligation, a commendable deference for public opinion, or a laudable zeal for public good, the base or foolish compliances of ambition, corruption or infatuation.

As avenues to foreign influence in innumerable ways, such attachments are particularly alarming to the truly enlightened and independent Patriot. How many opportunities do they afford to tamper with domestic factions, to practice the arts of seduction, to mislead public opinion, to influence or awe the public Councils! Such an attachment of a small or weak, towards a great and powerful Nation, dooms the former to be the satellite of the latter.

Against the insidious wiles of foreign influence, (I conjure you to believe me, fellow citizens) the jealousy of a free people ought to be *constantly* awake; since history and experience prove that foreign influence is one of the most baneful foes of Republican Government. But that jealousy to be useful must be impartial; else it becomes the instrument of the very influence to be avoided, instead of a defence against it. Excessive partiality for one foreign nation and excessive dislike of another, cause those whom they actuate to see danger only on one side, and serve to veil and even second the arts of influence on the other. Real Patriots, who may resist the intrigues of the favourite, are liable to become suspected and odious; while its tools and dupes usurp the applause and confidence of the people, to surrender their interests.

The Great rule of conduct for us, in regard to foreign Nations is in extending our commercial relations to have with them as little *political* connection as possible. So far as we have already formed engagements let them be fulfilled, with perfect good faith. Here let us stop.

Europe has a set of primary interests, which to us have none, or a very remote relation. Hence she must be engaged in frequent controversies, the causes of which are essentially foreign to our concerns. Hence therefore it must be unwise in us to implicate ourselves, by artificial ties, in the ordinary vicissitudes of her politics, or the ordinary combinations and collisions of her friendships, or enmities:

Our detached and distant situation invites and enables us to pursue a different course. If we remain one People, under an efficient government, the period is not far off, when we may defy material injury from external annoyance; when we may take such an attitude as will cause the neutrality we may at any time resolve upon to be scrupulously respected; when belligerent nations, under the impossibility of making acquisitions upon us, will not lightly hazard the giving us provocation; when we may choose peace or war, as our interest guided by our justice shall Counsel.

Why forego the advantages of so peculiar a situation? Why quit our own to stand upon foreign ground? Why, by interweaving our destiny with that of any part of Europe, entangle our peace and prosperity in the toils of European Ambition, Rivalship, Interest, Humour or Caprice?

'Tis our true policy to steer clear of permanent Alliances, with any portion of the foreign world. So far, I mean, as we are now at liberty to do it, for let me not be understood as capable of patronising infidility to existing engagements (I hold the maxim no less applicable to public than to private affairs, that honesty is always the best policy). I repeat it therefore, let those engagements be observed in their genuine sense. But in my opinion, it is unnecessary and would be unwise to extend them.

Taking care always to keep ourselves, by suitable establishments, on a respectably defensive posture, we may safely trust to temporary alliances for extraordinary emergencies.

Harmony, liberal intercourse with all Nations, are recommended by policy, humanity and interest. But even our Commercial policy should hold an equal and impartial hand: neither seeking nor granting exclusive favours or preferences; consulting the natural course of things; diffusing and deversifying by gentle means the streams of Commerce, but forcing nothing; establishing with Powers so disposed; in order to give to trade a stable course, to define the rights of our Merchants, and to enable the Government to support them; conventional rules of intercourse, the best that present circumstances and mutual opinion will permit, but temporary, and liable to be from time to time abandoned or varied, as experience and circumstances shall dictate; constantly keeping in view, that 'tis folly in one Nation to look for disinterested favors from another; that it must pay with a portion of its Independence for whatever it may accept under that character; that by such acceptance, it may place itself in the condition of having given equivalents for nominal favours and yet of being reproached with ingratitude for not giving more. There can be no greater error than to expect, or calculate upon real favors from Nation to Nation. 'Tis an illusion which experience must cure, which a just pride ought to discard.

In offering to you, my Countrymen these counsels of an old and affectionate friend, I dare not hope they will make the strong and lasting impression, I could wish; that they will controul the usual current of the passions, or prevent our Nation from running the course which has hitherto marked the Destiny of Nations: But if I may even flatter myself, that they may be productive of some partial benefit, some occasional good; that they may now and then recur to moderate the fury of party spirit, to warn against the mischiefs of foreign Intriegue, to guard against the Impostures of pretended patriotism; this hope will be a full recompence for the solicitude for your welfare, by which they have been dictated.

How far in the discharge of my Official duties, I have been guided by the principles which have been delineated, the public Records and other evidences of my conduct must Witness to You and to the world. To myself, the assurance of my own conscience is, that I have at least believed myself to be guided by them.

In relation to the still subsisting War in Europe, my Proclamation of the 22d. of April 1793 is in the index to my Plan. Sanctioned by your approving voice and by that of Your Representatives in both Houses of Congress, the spirit of that measure has continually governed me; uninfluenced by any attempts to deter or divert me from it.

After deliberate examination with the aid of the best lights I could obtain I was well satisfied that our Country, under all the circumstances of the case, had a right to take, and was bound in duty and interest, to take a Neutral position. Having taken it, I determined, as far as should depend upon me, to maintain it, with moderation, perseverance and firmness.

The considerations, which respect the right to hold this conduct, it is not necessary on this occasion to detail. I will only observe, that according to my understanding of the matter, that right, so far from being denied by any of the Belligerent Powers has been virtually admitted by all.

The duty of holding a Neutral conduct may be inferred, without any thing more, from the obligation which justice and humanity impose on every Nation, in cases in which it is free to act, to maintain inviolate the relations of Peace and amity towards other Nations.

The inducements of interest for observing that conduct will best be referred to your own reflections and experience. With me, a predominant motive has been to endeavour to gain time to our country to settle and mature its yet recent institutions, and to progress without interruption, to that degree of strength and consistency, which is necessary to give it, humanly speaking, the command of its own fortunes.

Though in reviewing the incidents of my Administration, I am unconscious of intentional error, I am nevertheless too sensible of my defects not to think it probable that I may have committed many errors. Whatever they may be I fervently beseech the Almighty to avert or mitigate the evils to which they may tend. I shall also carry with me the hope that my Country will never cease to view them with indulgence; and that after forty five years of my life dedicated to its Service, with an upright zeal, the faults of incompetent abilities will be consigned to oblivion, as myself must soon be to the Mansions of rest.

Relying on its kindness in this as in other things, and actuated by that fervent love towards it, which is so natural to a Man, who views in it the native soil of himself and his progenitors for several Generations; I anticipate with pleasing expectation that retreat, in which I promise myself to realize, without alloy, the sweet enjoyment of partaking, in the midst of my fellow Citizens, the benign influence of good Laws under a free Government, the ever favourite object of my heart, and the happy reward, as I trust, of our mutual cares, labours and dangers.

Fisher Ames

WASHINGTON: SYMBOL OF PUBLIC VIRTUE

Fisher Ames (1757–1808)—chief spokesman for the Federalists—was asked to deliver a eulogy on Washington shortly after the death of the former president. Using the occasion for political purposes, Ames gave an extremely partisan oration in which he praised Washington and criticized the Republicans. Washington was pictured as the personification not only of national virtue and honor but, more important, of Federalist idealism. To Ames, Washington's greatest achievement was not his military leadership, but his statesmanship. When the peace of America was threatened by the intrigues of France and the passions of his countrymen, Washington's patriotic devotion enabled him to lead the nation through the crisis. He brought order out of confusion, and, according to Ames, vindicated Federalist notions of good government.

How does Ames' notion of "public welfare" as presented in this selection differ from that in Washington's own statement? Does the difference reveal any misunderstood motives within the Federalists' own ranks?

SUCH a life as Washington's cannot derive honor from the circumstances of birth and education, though it throws back a lustre upon both. With an inquisitive mind, that always profited by the lights of others, and was unclouded by passions of its own, he acquired a maturity of judgment, rare in age, unparalleled in youth. Perhaps no young man had so early laid up a life's stock of materials for solid reflection, or settled so soon the principles and habits of his conduct. Gray experience listened to his counsels with respect, and at a time when youth is almost privileged to be rash, Virginia committed the safety of her frontier, and ultimately the safety of America, not merely to his valor, for that would be scarcely praise, but to his prudence.

It is not in Indian wars that heroes are celebrated; but it is there they are formed. No enemy can be more formidable, by the craft of his ambushes, the suddenness of his onset, or the ferocity of his vengeance. The soul of Washington was thus exercised to danger; and on the first trial, as on every other, it appeared firm in adversity, cool in action,

undaunted, self-possessed. His spirit, and still more his prudence, on the occasion of Braddock's defeat, diffused his name throughout America, and across the Atlantic. Even then his country viewed him with complacency, as her most hopeful son.

At the peace of 1763, Great Britain, in consequence of her victories, stood in a position to prescribe her own terms. She chose perhaps better for us than for herself; for by expelling the French from Canada we no longer feared hostile neighbors; and we soon found just cause to be afraid of our protectors. We discerned even then a truth, which the conduct of France has since so strongly confirmed, that there is nothing which the gratitude of weak states can give that will satisfy strong allies for their aid, but authority; nations that want protectors will have masters. Our settlements, no longer checked by enemies on the fronpier, rapidly increased; and it was discovered that America was growing to a size that could defend itself.

In this perhaps unforeseen, but at length obvious state of things, the British government conceived a jealousy of

From Seth Ames, ed., *Works of Fisher Ames* (Boston, 1854), Vol. II, pp. 73–88.

the colonies, of which, and of their intended measures of precaution, they made no secret.

Our nation, like its great leader, had only to take counsel from its courage. When Washington heard the voice of his country in distress, his obedience was prompt; and though his sacrifices were great, they cost him no effort. Neither the object nor the limits of my plan permit me to dilate on the military events of the revolutionary war. Our history is but a transcript of his claims on our gratitude: our hearts bear testimony, that they are claims not to be satisfied. When overmatched by numbers, a fugitive with a little band of faithful soldiers, the States as much exhausted as dismayed, he explored his own undaunted heart, and found there resources to retrieve our affairs. We have seen him display as much valor as gives fame to heroes, and as consummate prudence as insures success to valor; fearless of dangers that were personal to him, hesitating and cautious when they affected his country; preferring fame before safety or repose, and duty before fame.

Rome did not owe more to Fabius than America to Washington. Our nation shares with him the singular glory of having conducted a civil war with mildness, and a revolution with order.

The event of that war seemed to crown the felicity and glory both of America and its chief. Until that contest, a great part of the civilized world had been surprisingly ignorant of the force and character, and almost of the existence, of the British colonies. They had not retained what they knew, nor felt curiosity to know the state of thirteen wretched settlements, which vast woods inclosed, and still vaster woods divided from each other. They did not view the colonists so much a people as a race of fugitives, whom want, and solitude, and intermixture with the savages, had made barbarians.

At this time, while Great Britain wielded a force truly formidable to the most powerful states, suddenly, astonished Europe beheld a feeble people, till then unknown, stand forth, and defy this giant to the combat. It was so un-

equal, all expected it would be short. Our final success exalted their admiration to its highest point: they allowed to Washington all that is due to transcendent virtue, and to the Americans more than is due to human nature. They considered us a race of Washingtons, and admitted that nature in America was fruitful only in prodigies. Their books and their travellers, exaggerating and distorting all their representations, assisted to establish the opinion, that this is a new world, with a new order of men and things adapted to it; that here we practise industry, amidst the abundance that requires none; that we have morals so refined, that we do not need laws; and though we have them, yet we ought to consider their execution as an insult and a wrong; that we have virtue without weaknesses, sentiment without passions, and liberty without factions. These illusions, in spite of their absurdity, and perhaps because they are absurd enough to have dominion over the imagination only, have been received by many of the malecontents against the governments of Europe, and induced them to emigrate. Such allusions are too soothing to vanity to be entirely checked in their currency among Americans.

They have been pernicious, as they cherish false ideas of the right of men and the duties of rulers. They have led the citizens to look for liberty, where it is not; and to consider the government, which is its castle, as its prison.

Washington retired to Mount Vernon, and the eyes of the world followed him. He left his countrymen to their simplicity and their passions, and their glory soon departed. Europe began to be undeceived, and it seemed for a time, as if, by the acquisition of independence, our citizens were disappointed. The confederation was then the only compact made "to form a perfect union of the States, to establish justice, to insure the tranquillity, and provide for the security of the nation;" and accordingly, union was a name that still commanded reverence, though not obedience. The system called justice, was, in some of the States, iniquity reduced to elementary principles; and the public tranquillity was such a portentous calm, as rings in deep caverns before the explosion of an earthquake. Most of the States then were in fact, though not in form, unbalanced democracies. Reason, it is true, spoke audibly in their constitutions; passion and prejudice louder in their laws. It is to the honor of Massachusetts, that it is chargeable with little deviation from principles; its adherence to them was one of the causes of a dangerous rebellion. It was scarcely possible that such governments should not be agitated by parties, and that prevailing parties should not be vindictive and unjust. Accordingly, in some of the States, creditors were treated as outlaws; bankrupts were armed with legal authority to be persecutors; and by the shock of all confidence and faith, society was shaken to its foundations. Liberty we had, but we dreaded its abuse almost as much as its loss; and the wise, who deplored the one, clearly foresaw the other.

The peace of America hung by a thread, and factions were already sharpening their weapons to cut it. The project of three separate empires in America was beginning to be broached, and the progress of licentiousness would have soon rendered her citizens unfit for liberty in either of them. An age of blood and misery would have punished our disunion; but these were not the considerations to deter ambition from its purpose, while there were so many circumstances in our political situation to favor it.

At this awful crisis, which all the wise so much dreaded at the time, yet which appears, on a retrospect, so much more dreadful than their fears; some man was wanting who possessed a commanding power over the popular passions, but over whom those passions had no power. That man was Washington.

His name, at the head of such a list of worthies as would reflect honor on any country, had its proper weight with all the enlightened, and with almost all the well-disposed among the less informed citizens, and, blessed be God! the Constitution was adopted. Yes, to the eternal honor of America among the nations of the earth, it was adopted, in spite of the obstacles, which in any other country, and perhaps in any other age of *this*, would have been insurmountable; in spite of the doubts and fears, which well-meaning prejudice creates for itself, and which party so artfully inflames into stubbornness; in spite of the vice, which it has subjected to restraint, and which is therefore its immortal and implacable foe; in spite of the oligarchies in some of the States, from whom it snatched dominion;—it was adopted, and our country enjoys one more invaluable chance for its union and happiness: invaluable! if the retrospect of the dangers we have escaped shall sufficiently inculcate the principles we have so tardily established. Perhaps multitudes are not to be taught by their fears only, without suffering much to deepen the impression; for experience brandishes in her school a whip of scorpions, and teaches nations her summary lessons of wisdom by the scars and wounds of their adversity.

The amendments which have been projected in some of the States show, that in them, at least, these lessons are not well remembered. In a confederacy of States, some powerful, others weak, the weakness of the federal union will sooner or later encourage, and will not restrain, the ambition and injustice of the members: the weak can no otherwise be strong or safe, but in the energy of the national government. It is this defect, which the blind jealousy of the weak States not unfrequently contributes to prolong, that has proved fatal to all the confederations that ever existed.

Although it was impossible that such merit as Washington's should not produce envy, it was scarcely possible that, with such a transcendent reputation, he should have rivals. Accordingly, he was unanimously chosen President of the United States.

As a general and a patriot, the measure of his glory was already full; there was no fame left for him to excel but his own; and even that task, the mightiest of all his labors, his civil magistracy has accomplished.

No sooner did the new government begin its auspicious course, than order seemed to arise out of confusion. Commerce and industry awoke, and were cheerful at their labors; for credit and confidence awoke with them. Everywhere was the appearance of prosperity; and the only fear was, that its progress was too rapid to consist with the purity and simplicity of ancient manners. The cares and labors of the president were incessant; his exhortations, example, and authority, were employed to excite zeal and activity for the public service; able officers were selected, only for their merits; and some of them remarkably distinguished themselves by their successful management of the public business. Government was administered with such integrity, without mystery, and in so prosperous a course, that it seemed to be wholly employed in acts of beneficence. Though it has made many thousand malcontents, it has never, by its rigor or injustice, made one man wretched.

Such was the state of public affairs; and did it not seem perfectly to ensure uninterrupted harmony to the citizens? Did they not, in respect to their government and its administration, possess their whole heart's desire? They had seen and suffered long the want of an efficient constitution; they had freely ratified it; they saw Washington, their tried friend, the father of his country, invested with its powers; they knew that he could not exceed or betray them, without forfeiting his own reputation. Consider, for a moment, what a reputation it was; such as no man ever before possessed by so clear a title, and in so high a degre.. His fame seemed in its purity to exceed even its brightness. Office took honor from his acceptance, but conferred none. Ambition stood awed and darkened by his shadow. For where, through the wide earth, was the man so vain as to dispute precedence with him; or what were the honors that could make the possessor Washington's superior? Refined and complex as the ideas of virtue are, even the gross could discern in his life the infinite superiority of her rewards. Mankind perceived some change in their ideas of greatness; the splendor of power, and even of the name of con-

queror, had grown dim in their eyes. They did not know that Washington could augment his fame; but they knew and felt, that the world's wealth, and its empire too, would be a bribe far beneath his acceptance.

This is not exaggeration; never was confidence in a man and a chief magistrate more widely diffused, or more solidly established.

If it had been in the nature of man, that we should enjoy liberty, without the agitations of party, the United States had a right, under these circumstances, to expect it; but it was impossible. Where there is no liberty, they may be exempt from party. It will seem strange, but it scarcely admits a doubt, that there are fewer malcontents in Turkey than in any free state in the world. Where the people have no power, they enter into no contests, and are not anxious to know how they shall use it. The spirit of discontent becomes torpid for want of employment, and sighs itself to rest. The people sleep soundly in their chains, and do not even dream of their weight. They lose their turbulence with their energy, and become as tractable as any other animals; a state of degradation, in which they extort our scorn, and engage our pity, for the misery they do not feel. Yet that heart is a base one, and fit only for a slave's bosom, that would not bleed freely, rather than submit to such a condition; for liberty, with all its parties and agitations, is more desirable than slavery. Who would not prefer the republics of ancient Greece, where liberty once subsisted in its excess, its delirium, terrible in its charms, and glistening to the last with the blaze of the very fire that consumed it?

I do not know that I ought, but I am sure that I do, prefer those republics to the dozing slavery of the modern Greece, where the degraded wretches have suffered scorn till they merit it, where they tread on classic ground, on the ashes of heroes and patriots, unconscious of their ancestry, ignorant of the nature and almost of the name of liberty and insensible even to the passion for it. Who, on this contrast, can forbear to say, it is the modern Greece that lies buried, that sleeps forgotten in the caves of Turkish darkness? It is the ancient Greece that lives in remembrance, that is still bright with glory, still fresh in immortal youth. They are unworthy of liberty who entertain a less exalted idea of its excellence. The misfortune is, that those who profess to be its most passionate admirers have, generally, the least comprehension of its hazards and impediments; they expect that an enthusiastic admiration of its nature will reconcile the multitude to the irksomeness of its restraints. Delusive expectation! Washington was not thus deluded. We have his solemn warning against the often fatal propensities of liberty. He had reflected, that men are often false to their country and their honor, false to duty and even to their interest, but multitudes of men are never long false or deaf to their passions; these will find obstacles in the laws, associates in party. The fellowships thus formed are more intimate, and impose commands more imperious, than those of society.

Thus party forms a state within the state, and is animated by a rivalship, fear, and hatred, of its superior. When this happens, the merits of the government will become fresh provocations and offences, for they are the merits of an enemy. No wonder then, that as soon as party found the virtue and glory of Washington were obstacles, the attempt was made, by calumny, to surmount them both. For this, the greatest of all his trials, we know that he was prepared. He knew that the government must possess sufficient strength from within or without, or fall a victim to faction. This *interior* strength was plainly inadequate to its defence, unless it could be reinforced from *without* by the zeal and patriotism of the citizens; and this latter resource was certainly as accessible to President Washington as to any chief magistrate that ever lived. The life of the federal government, he considered, was in the breath of the people's nostrils; whenever they should happen to be so infatuated or inflamed as to abandon its defence, its end must be as speedy, and might be as tragical, as a constitution for France.

While the president was thus administering the government in so wise and just a manner, as to engage the great majority of the enlightened and virtuous citizens to coöperate with him for its support, and while he indulged the hope that time and habit were confirming their attachment, the French Revolution had reached that point in its progress, when its terrible principles began to agitate all civilized nations. I will not, on this occasion, detain you to express, though my thoughts teem with it, my deep abhorrence of that revolution; its despotism by the mob or the military from the first, and its hypocrisy of morals to the last. Scenes have passed there which exceed description, and which, for other reasons, I will not attempt to describe; for it would not be possible, even at this distance of time, and with the sea between us and France, to go through with the recital of them without perceiving horror gather, like a frost, about the heart and almost stop its pulse. That revolution has been constant in nothing but its vicissitudes and its promises; always delusive, but always renewed to establish philosophy by crimes and liberty by the sword. The people of France, if they are not like the modern Greeks, find their cap of liberty is a soldier's helmet; and with all their imitation of dictators and consuls, their exactest similitude to these Roman ornaments is in their chains. The nations of Europe perceive another resemblance in their all-conquering ambition.

But it is only the influence of that event on America, and on the measures of the president that belongs to my subject. It would be ungratefully wrong to his character, to be silent in respect to a part of it, which has the most signally illustrated his virtues.

The genuine character of that revolution is not even yet so well understood as the dictates of self-preservation require it should be. The chief duty and care of all governments is to protect the rights of property, and the tranquillity of society. The leaders of the French revolution from the beginning excited the poor against the rich. This has made the rich poor, but it will never make the poor rich. On the contrary, they were used only as blind instruments to make those leaders masters, first of the adverse party, and then of the state. Thus the powers of the state were turned round into a direction exactly contrary to the proper one, not to preserve tranquillity and restrain violence, but to excite violence by the lure of power and plunder and vengeance. Thus all France has been, and still is, as much the prize of the ruling party as a captured ship, and if any right or possession has escaped confiscation, there is none that has not been liable to it.

Thus it clearly appears, that in its origin, its character, and its means, the government of that country is revolutionary; that is, not only different from, but directly contrary to, every regular and well-ordered society. It is a danger, similar in its kind, and at least equal in degree, to that with which ancient Rome menaced her enemies. The allies of Rome were slaves; and it cost some hundred years' efforts of her policy and arms to make her enemies her allies. Nations at this day can trust no better to treaties; they cannot even trust to arms unless they are used with a spirit and perseverance becoming the magnitude of their danger. For the French Revolution has been from the first hostile to all right and justice, to all peace and order in society; and therefore its very existence has been a state of warfare against the civilized world, and most of all against free and orderly republics, for such are never without factions, ready to be the allies of France, and to aid her in the work of destruction. Accordingly, scarcely any but republics have they subverted. Such governments, by showing in practice what republican liberty is, detect French imposture, and show what their pretexts are not.

To subvert them, therefore, they had, besides the facility that faction affords, the double excitement of removing a reproach, and converting their greatest obstacles into their most efficient auxiliaries.

Who, then, on careful reflection, will be surprised that the French and their partisans instantly conceived the desire, and made the most powerful attempts, to revolutionize the American government? But it will hereafter seem strange that their excesses should be excused as the effects of a struggle for liberty; and that so many of our citizens should be flattered, while they were insulted with the idea that our example was copied and our principles pursued. Nothing was ever more false or more fascinating. Our liberty depends on our education, our laws and habits, to which even prejudices yield; on the dispersion of our people on farms, and on the almost equal diffusion of property; it is founded on morals and religion, whose authority reigns in the heart; and on the influence all these produce on public opinion, before that opinion governs rulers. Here liberty is restraint; there it is violence; here it is mild and cheering, like the morning sun of our summer, brightening the hills and making the valleys green; there it is like the sun, when his rays dart pestilence on the sands of Africa. American liberty calms and restrains the licentious passions, like an angel, that says to the winds and troubled seas, be still; but how has French licentiousness appeared to the wretched citizens of Switzerland and Venice? Do not their haunted imaginations, even when they wake, represent her as a monster, with eyes that flash wildfire, hands that hurl thunderbolts, a voice that shakes the foundation of the hills? She stands, and her ambition measures the earth; she speaks, and an epidemic fury seizes the nations.

Experience is lost upon us if we deny that it had seized a large part of the American nation. It is as sober and intelligent, as free and as worthy to be free as any in the world; yet like all other people we have passions and prejudices, and they had received a violent impulse, which for a time misled us.

Jacobinism had become here, as in France, rather a sect than a party, inspiring a fanaticism that was equally intolerant and contagious. The delusion was general enough to be thought the voice of the people, therefore claiming authority without proof, and jealous enough to exact acquiescence without a murmur of contradiction. Some progress was made in training multitudes to be vindictive and ferocious. To them nothing seemed amiable but the revolutionary justice of Paris; nothing terrible but the government and justice of America. The very name of *patriots* was claimed and applied in proportion as the citizens had alienated their hearts from America, and transferred their affections to their foreign corrupter. Party discerned its intimate connection of interest with France, and consummated its profligacy by yielding to foreign influence.

The views of these allies required that this country should engage in war with Great Britain. Nothing less would give to France all the means of annoying this dreaded rival; nothing less would ensure the subjection of America, as a satellite to the ambition of France; nothing else could make a revolution here perfectly inevitable.

For this end the minds of the citizens were artfully inflamed, and the moment was watched and impatiently waited for, when their long-heated passions should be in fusion to pour them forth, like the lava of a volcano, to blacken and consume the peace and government of our country.

The systematic operations of a faction, under foreign influence, had begun to appear, and were successively pursued, in a manner too deeply alarming to be soon forgotten. Who of us does not remember this worst of evils in this worst of ways? Shame would forget, if it could, that in one of the States amendments were proposed to break down the federal Senate, which, as in the State governments, is a great bulwark of the public order. To break down another, an extravagant judiciary power was claimed for States. In another State a rebellion was fomented by the agent of France; and who, without fresh indignation, can remember that the powers of government were openly usurped, troops levied, and ships fitted out to fight for her? Nor can any true friend to our government consider, without dread, that soon afterwards, the treaty-making

power was boldly challenged for a branch of the government, from which the Constitution has wisely withholden it.

I am oppressed, and know not how to proceed with my subject. Washington, blessed be God! who endued him with wisdom and clothed him with power; Washington issued his proclamation of neutrality, and at an early period arrested the intrigues of France and the passions of his countrymen, on the very edge of the precipice of war and revolution.

This act of firmness, at the hazard of his reputation and peace, entitles him to the name of the first of patriots. Time was gained for the citizens to recover their virtue and good sense, and they soon recovered them. The crisis was passed and America was saved.

You and I, most respected fellow-citizens, should be sooner tired than satisfied in recounting the particulars of this illustrious man's life.

How great he appeared while he administered the government, how much greater when he retired from it, how he accepted the chief military command under his wise and upright successor, how his life was unspotted like his fame, and how his death was worthy of his life, are so many distinct subjects of instruction, and each of them singly more than enough for an elogium. I leave the task, however, to history and to posterity; they will be faithful to it.

It is not impossible that some will affect to consider the honors paid to this great patriot by the nation as excessive, idolatrous, and degrading to freemen, who are all equal. I answer, that refusing to virtue its legitimate honors would not prevent their being lavished in future, on any worthless and ambitious favorite. If this day's example should have its natural effect, it will be salutary. Let such honors be so conferred only when, in future, they shall be so merited; then the public sentiment will not be misled, nor the principles of a just equality corrupted. The best evidence of reputation is a man's whole life. We have now, alas! all Washington's before us. There has scarcely appeared a really great man whose character has been more admired in his lifetime, or less correctly understood by his admirers. When it is comprehended, it is no easy task to delineate its excellences in such a manner as to give to the portrait both interest and resemblance; for it requires thought and study to understand the true ground of the superiority of his character over many others, whom he resembled in the principles of action, and even in the manner of acting. But perhaps he excels all the great men that ever lived, in the steadiness of his adherence to his maxims of life, and in the uniformity of all his conduct to the same maxims. These maxims, though wise, were yet not so remarkable for their wisdom as for their authority over his life; for if there were any errors in his judgment, (and he discovered as few as any man,) we know of no blemishes in his virtue. He was the patriot without reproach; he loved his country well enough to hold his success in serving it an ample recompense. Thus far self-love and love of country coincided; but when his country needed sacrifices that no other man could or perhaps would be willing to make, he did not even hesitate. This was virtue in its most exalted character. More than once he put his fame at hazard, when he had reason to think it would be sacrificed, at least in this age. Two instances cannot be denied; when the army was disbanded; and again, when he stood, like Leonidas at the pass of Thermopylae, to defend our independence against France.

It is indeed almost as difficult to draw his character as the portrait of virtue. The reasons are similar; our ideas of moral excellence are obscure, because they are complex, and we are obliged to resort to illustrations. Washington's example is the happiest to show what virtue is; and to delineate his character we naturally expatiate on the beauty of virtue; much must be felt and much imagined. His preëminence is not so much to be seen in the display of any one virtue as in the possession of them all, and in the practice of the most difficult.

Hereafter, therefore, his character must be studied before it will be striking; and then it will be admitted as a model, a precious one to a free republic.

It is no less difficult to speak of his talents. They were adapted to lead, without dazzling mankind; and to draw forth and employ the talents of others, without being misled by them. In this he was certainly superior, that he neither mistook nor misapplied his own. His great modesty and reserve would have concealed them, if great occasions had not called them forth; and then, as he never spoke from the affectation to shine, nor acted from any sinister motives, it is from their effects only that we are to judge of their greatness and extent. In public trusts, where men, acting conspicuously, are cautious, and in those private concerns, where few conceal or resist their weaknesses, Washington was uniformly great, pursuing right conduct from right maxims. His talents were such as assist a sound judgment, and ripen with it. His prudence was consummate, and seemed to take the direction of his powers and passions; for as a soldier, he was more solicitous to avoid mistakes that might be fatal, than to perform exploits that are brilliant; and as a statesman, to adhere to just principles, however old, than to pursue novelties; and therefore, in both characters, his qualities were singularly adapted to the interest, and were tried in the greatest perils, of the country. His habits of inquiry were so far remarkable, that he was never satisfied with investigating, nor desisted from it, so long as he had less than all the light that he could obtain upon a subject, and then he made his decision without bias.

This command over the partialities that so generally stop men short, or turn them aside in their pursuit of truth, is one of the chief causes of his unvaried course of right conduct in so many difficult scenes, where every human actor must be presumed to err. If he had strong passions, he had learned to subdue them, and to be moderate and mild. If he had weaknesses, he concealed them, which is rare, and excluded them from the government of his temper and conduct, which is still more rare. If he loved fame, he never made improper compliances for what is called popularity. The fame he enjoyed is of the kind that will last forever; yet it was rather the effect, than the motive, of his conduct. Some future Plutarch will search for a parallel to his character. Epaminondas is perhaps the brightest name of all antiquity. Our Washington resembled him in the purity and ardor of his patriotism; and like him, he first exalted the glory of his country. There it is to be hoped the parallel ends; for Thebes fell with Epaminondas. But such comparisons cannot be pursued far, without departing from the similitude. For we shall find it is difficult to compare great men as great rivers; some we admire for the length and rapidity of their current, and the grandeur of their cataracts; others, for the majestic silence and fulness of their streams: we cannot bring them together to measure the difference of their waters. The unambitious life of Washington, declining fame, yet courted by it, seemed, like the Ohio, to choose its long way through solitudes, diffusing fertility; or, like his own Potomac, widening and deepening his channel, as he approaches the sea, and displaying most the usefulness and serenity of his greatness towards the end of his course. Such a citizen would do honor to any country. The constant veneration and affection of his country will show, that it was worthy of such a citizen.

However his military fame may excite the wonder of mankind, it is chiefly by his civil magistracy, that his example will instruct them. Great generals have arisen in all ages of the world, and perhaps most in those of despotism and darkness. In times of violence and convulsion, they rise by the force of the whirlwind, high enough to ride in it, and direct the storm. Like meteors, they glare on the black clouds with a splendor that, while it dazzles and terrifies, makes nothing visible but the darkness. The fame of heroes is indeed growing vulgar; they multiply in every long war; they stand in history, and thicken in their ranks, almost as undistinguished as their own soldiers.

But such a chief magistrate as Washington, appears like the polestar in a clear sky, to direct the skilful statesman. His presidency will form an epoch, and be distinguished as the age of Washington. Already it assumes its high place in the political region. Like the milky way, it whitens along its allotted portion of the hemisphere. The latest generations of men will survey, through the telescope of history, the space where so many virtues blend their rays, and delight to separate them into groups and distinct virtues. As the best illustration of them, the living monument, to which the first of patriots would have chosen to consign his fame, it is my earnest prayer to heaven, that our country may subsist, even to that late day, in the plenitude of its liberty and happiness, and mingle its mild glory with Washington's.

Robert Goodloe Harper

THE FEDERALISTS AS REALISTS

Robert Goodloe Harper (c. 1765–1825) arrived in Congress in 1795, and, after paying homage to Madison and Jefferson, had been expected to enter the Republican ranks. Within a few months, however, he reversed his position completely and became the most partisan of Federalists. Harper argued later that the Federalists' main concern had been the creation of a centralized national government rather than a fragmented federal system. To achieve this goal the Federalists had to make the central government independent of the state governments, to render the executive branch superior to the legislative arm, and to elect to Congress men of talent who would place public service above private gain.

THE leading principle of their system, as to foreign nations, has been to preserve peace and amity with all, by a conduct just liberal and fair towards all; but to grant privileges to none, and to submit to indignities from none; to rely for the protection of our rights and honour, not on the friendship the justice or the forbearance of other governments, but on our own strength and resources; to employ vigorous means for calling forth those resources, and preparing them for exertion in time of need; to hold the olive branch in one hand and the sword in the other; to employ peaceable means for attaining our just objects, while peaceable means could afford rational hopes of success; and to shew ourselves ready to resort to force, should those hopes be found fallacious.

Regulating its conduct by these maxims, the government of the United States under the direction of the federalists, with Washington and afterwards Adams at their head, has preserved the nation in peace, through the most general and the most furious war that has afflicted the world in modern times. . . .

*   *   *

In the management of our domestic affairs their system has been, in the first place to support vigourously the independence and authority of the federal government; which alone is capable of ensuring our safety from abroad, by opposing to foreign nations the barrier of our united strength, and of maintaining our peace at home, by checking the ambition and repressing the passions of the several states, and balancing their forces, so as to prevent the greater from overpowering and subduing the lesser. They well knew this government, being under the necessity of laying and collecting considerable taxes, of raising and supporting armies and fleets, of maintaining numerous officers, and of carrying on all those expensive operations which its superintendance of our general affairs require, and from which the state governments are wholly exempt, is far more likely than those governments to incur unpopularity, to become subject to the imputation of extravagance, oppression and ambitious views, and to be deprived of the public confidence. They well knew that this government, being removed to a greater distance than the state governments from the people, was more apt to be viewed with jealousy and considered as a foreign government; and that there never would be wanting ambitious and restless men, who failing to obtain that share of influence in the federal government, or those honours and employments under it, to which they

From Robert Goodloe Harper, *Select Works* (Baltimore, 1814), Vol. I, pp. 327–350.

might think themselves entitled, would take refuge in the state governments, and avail themselves of all these circumstances to render the federal government odious, to excite against it the public resentment, and even to over-rule and controul it by means of the state governments. Well knowing this, the federalists considered it as a principle of the utmost importance for the preservation of the federal government, to render it as independent as possible of state influence; to give it a movement of its own, and complete power to enforce its own laws; to resist state encroachments; and to restrain the state governments within their just and proper bounds. In every struggle between the federal and the state governments, they considered the latter as possessing infinitely the greatest natural strength; and therefore thought it their duty to take part with the former in order to preserve the balance.

As to the federal government itself, their second great maxim was to support the executive power, against the encroachments, the ambition, and the superior strength of the popular branch. The power of a popular assembly, being little suspected by the people, is always little watched; and as no one member is to bear the blame of any excesses which the whole body may commit, its power is but little restrained by personal responsibility and a regard to character, and of course is very likely to be abused. Hence has resulted, in every age and nation where the form of government admitted popular assemblies, a constant effort on the part of those assemblies to get all power into their own hands, and to exercise it according to their own passions and caprice. This has every where produced the necessity of checking the power of those assemblies, by confining it wholly to legislation, by dividing it between two houses, and by given the judicial and executive powers to persons independent of the legislature. This has been done by our constitution; which gives the executive power to the President, a single magistrate, places the judicial power in the courts, and divides the legislative power between the Senate and House of Representatives. This House of Representatives, being the most numerous and the most popular body, is subject to the same passions and dispositions which popular bodies ever feel; and consequently has a perpetual tendency to encroach on the executive powers, and to direct and controul the President in the exercise of his authority. As the President, being a single magistrate, is much more apt to be suspected and viewed with a jealous eye than this popular assembly, which the people consider as nearer to themselves and more under their controul, he would have the people against him in these contests, and must finally submit absolutely to the controul of the House, were there not always some members of it, whose just way of thinking and regard to the constitution induce them to oppose the improper enterprizes of their own body, and to defend the executive power against its perpetual attacks. This was the conduct of the federalists. Knowing the executive power to be absolutely essential for preserving the due balance of the constitution, and for conducting the affairs of the nation with prudence steadiness and success, and knowing it also to be in itself much weaker than its antagonist; they made themselves its defenders, and by their perseverance and talents have thus far succeeded, in preserving to it the weight and authority designed for it by the constitution.

It was a third maxim in the system of the federalists, to give liberal not large compensations to men in office: well knowing that in a country where there are but few fortunes, and where almost every man of talents and character depends on his industry for supporting and providing for his family, the contrary system has a constant and powerful tendency, to throw the most important offices into the hands of unworthy or unqualified persons, who either neglect or mismanage the public business, or resort to dishonest means for supplying the deficiencies in their regular compensation. Nothing is more true, than that men of talents and character will not long leave their homes and devote their time to the public service, unless they are at least supported decently; and that if we wish for able and faithful services we may pay their price. This the federal government has never done. The first officers under it do not receive enough to support them and their families in a proper manner. Hence in part the difficulty which has been constantly experienced, in prevailing on men of high character and qualifications to fill those offices. The Secretary of State for instance, or the Secretary of the Treasury, receives but little more from his office, than half as much as a lawyer of talents can derive from his practice, with half the labour and confinement. The federalists have constantly endeavoured to remedy this abuse. They have done some thing but never were able to do enough. The expense is constantly made an objection; but it is a most futile objection. To compensate liberally and even handsomely all the principal officers of the government, would require an additional expense of perhaps thirty thousand dollars annually; which is less than a man without talents, in one of those offices, may waste or lose through mismanagement in a month. . . .

*   *   *

Such have been the principles and measures of the federalists, such their political system, and such its results. By those results they wish to be judged. In that book which their principles led them to venerate it is written, that a tree shall be judged by its fruits. By their fruits let them be judged; and they do not fear the decision.

Fisher Ames

THE FEDERALISTS AS IDEOLOGUES

Fisher Ames argued passionately that his party had been motivated by idealism during the 1790's, while the Republicans had remained realists. The Federalists' major flaw, according to Ames, was their excessive idealism. Believing in public virtue and patriotism, the Federalists had misjudged the American people, Ames said, and therefore had been doomed to defeat. The Republicans, on the other hand, had appealed to the baser instincts of the people—to their greed, passions, and depravity—and had won in 1800. Thus true liberty had been overcome by the malignant spirit of democracy; but Ames insisted, "a democracy cannot last . . . its nature ordains that its next change shall be into military despotism." Taking a cyclical view of history, Ames felt that the American republic, like the republic of Rome, would fall into the hands of a dictator when the people tired of the anarchy that would result from the rule of Republican demagogues.

THE great object, then, of political wisdom in framing our Constitution, was to guard against licentiousness, that inbred malady of democracies, that deforms their infancy with gray hairs and decrepitude.

The federalists relied much on the efficiency of an independent judiciary, as a check on the hasty turbulence of the popular passions. They supposed the senate, proceeding from the states, and chosen for six years, would form a sort of balance to the democracy, and realize the hope that a federal republic of states might subsist. They counted much on the information of the citizens; that they would give their unremitted attention to public affairs; that either dissensions would not arise in our happy country, or if they should, that the citizens would remain calm, and would walk, like the three Jews in Nebuchadnezzar's furnace, unharmed amidst the fires of party.

It is needless to ask how rational such hopes were, or how far experience has verified them.

The progress of party has given to Virginia, a preponderance that perhaps was not foreseen. Certainly, since the late amendment in the article for the choice of president and vice-president, there is no existing provision of any efficacy to counteract it.

The project of arranging states in a federal union has long been deemed, by able writers and statesmen, more promising than the scheme of a single republic. The experiment, it has been supposed, has not yet been fairly tried; and much has been expected from the example of America.

If states were neither able nor inclined to obstruct the federal union, much indeed might be hoped from such a confederation. But Virginia, Pennsylvania, and New York are of an extent sufficient to form potent monarchies, and of course are too powerful, as well as too proud, to be subjects of the federal laws. Accordingly, one of the first schemes of amendment, and the most early executed, was to exempt them in form from the obligations of justice. States are not liable to be sued. Either the federal head or the powerful members must govern. Now, as it is a thing ascertained by experience that the great states are not

From Seth Ames, ed., *Works of Fisher Ames* (Boston, 1854), Vol. II, pp. 349–350, 354–356, 359, 361–363, 365–366, 368–382, 387, 390–399.

willing, and cannot be compelled to obey the union, it is manifest that their ambition is most singularly invited to aspire to the usurpation or control of the powers of the confederacy. A confederacy of many states, all of them small in extent and population, not only might not obstruct, but happily facilitate the federal authority. But the late presidential amendment demonstrates the overwhelming preponderance of several great states, combining together to engross the control of federal affairs.

* * *

But there are not many, perhaps not five hundred, even among the federalists, who yet allow themselves to view the progress of licentiousness as so speedy, so sure, and so fatal, as the deplorable experience of our country shows that it is, and the evidence of history and the constitution of human nature demonstrate that it must be.

The truth is, such an opinion, admitted with all the terrible light of its proof, no less shocks our fears than our vanity, no less disturbs our quiet than our prejudices. We are summoned by the tocsin to every perilous and painful duty. Our days are made heavy with the pressure of anxiety, and our nights restless with visions of horror. We listen to the clank of chains, and overhear the whispers of assassins. We mark the barbarous dissonance of mingled rage and triumph in the yell of an infatuated mob; we see the dismal glare of their burnings and scent the loathsome steam of human victims offered in sacrifice.

These reflections may account for the often lamented blindness, as well as apathy of our well-disposed citizens. Who would choose to study the tremendous records of the fates, or to remain long in the dungeon of the furies? Who that is penetrating enough to foresee our scarcely hidden destiny, is hardy enough to endure its anxious contemplation?

It may not long be more safe to disturb than it is easy to enlighten the democratic faith in regard to our political propensities, since it will neither regard what is obvious, nor yield to the impression of events, even after they have happened. The thoughtless and ignorant care for nothing but the name of liberty, which is as much the end as the instrument of party, and equally fills up the measure of their comprehension and desires. According to the conception of such men, the public liberty can never perish; it will enjoy immortality, like the dead in the memory of the living. . . .

This very opinion in regard to the destinies of our country is neither less extensively diffused, nor less solidly established. Such men will persist in thinking our liberty cannot be in danger till it is irretrievably lost. It is even the boast of multitudes that our system of government is a pure democracy.

What is there left that can check its excesses or retard the velocity of its fall? Not the control of the several states, for they already whirl in the vortex of faction; and of consequence, not the senate, which is appointed by the states. Surely not the judiciary, for we cannot expect the office of the priesthood from the victim at the altar. Are we to be sheltered by the force of ancient manners? Will this be sufficient to control the two evil spirits of license and innovation? Where is any vestige of those manners left, but in New England? And even in New England their authority is contested and their purity debased. Are our civil and religious institutions to stand so firmly as to sustain themselves and so much of the fabric of the public order as is propped by their support? On the contrary, do we not find the ruling faction in avowed hostility to our religious institutions? In effect, though not in form, their protection is abandoned by our laws and confided to the steadiness of sentiment and fashion; and if they are still powerful auxiliaries of lawful authority, it is owing to the tenaciousness with which even a degenerate people maintain their habits, and to a yet remaining, though impaired veneration for the maxims of our ancestors.

We are changing, and if democracy triumphs in New England, it is to be apprehended that in a few years we shall be as prone to disclaim our great progenitors, as they, if they should return again to the earth, with grief and shame to disown their degenerate descendants.

Is the turbulence of our democracy to be restrained by preferring to the magistracy only the grave and upright, the men who profess the best moral and religious principles, and whose lives bear testimony in favor of their profession, whose virtues inspire confidence, whose services, gratitude, and whose talents command admiration? Such magistrates would add dignity to the best government, and disarm the malignity of the worst. But the bare moving of this question will be understood as a sarcasm by men of both parties. The powers of impudence itself are scarcely adequate to say that our magistrates are such men. . . .

It never has happened in the world, and it never will, that a democracy has been kept out of the control of the fiercest and most turbulent spirits in the society; they will breathe into it all their own fury, and make it subservient to the worst designs of the worst men. . . .

*   *   *

Yet, as if there were neither vice nor passion in the world, one of the loudest of our boasts, one of the dearest of all the tenets of our creed is, that we are a sovereign people, self-governed—it would be nearer truth to say, self-conceited. For in what sense is it true that any people, however free, are self-governed? If they have in fact no government but such as comports with their ever-varying and often inordinate desires, then it is anarchy; if it counteracts those desires, it is compulsory. The individual who is left to act according to his own humor is not governed at all; and if any considerable number, and especially any combination of individuals, find or can place themselves in this situation, then the society is no longer free. For liberty obviously consists in the salutary restraint, and not in the uncontrolled indulgence of such humors. Now of all desires, none will so much need restraint, or so impatiently endure it, as those of the ambitious, who will form factions, first to elude, then to rival, and finally to usurp the powers of the state; and of the sons of vice, who are the enemies of law, because no just law can be their friend. The first want to govern the state; and the others, that the state should not govern them. A sense of common interest will soon incline these two original factions of every free state to coalesce into one. . . .

*   *   *

The theory of a democracy supposes that the will of the people ought to prevail, and that, as the majority possess not only the better right, but the superior force, of course it will prevail. A greater force, they argue, will inevitably overcome a less. When a constitution provides, with an imposing solemnity of detail, for the collection of the opinions of a majority of the citizens, every sanguine reader not only becomes assured that the will of the people must prevail, but he goes further, and refuses to examine the reasons, and to excuse the incivism and presumption of those who can doubt of this inevitable result. Yet common sense and our own recent experience have shown, that a combination of a very small minority can effectually defeat the authority of the national will. The votes of a majority may sometimes, though not invariably, show what ought to be done; but to awe or subdue the force of a thousand men, the government must call out the superior force of two thousand men. It is therefore established the very instant it is brought to the test, that the mere will of a majority is inefficient and without authority. And as to employing a superior force to procure obedience, which a democratic government has an undoubted right to do, and so indeed has every other, it is obvious that the admitted necessity of this resort completely overthrows all the boasted advantages of the democratic system. For if obedience cannot be procured by reason, it must be obtained by compulsion; and this is exactly what every other government will do in a like case.

Still, however, the friends of the democratic theory will maintain that this dire resort to force will be exceedingly rare, because the public reason will be more clearly expressed and more respectfully understood than under any other form of government. The citizens will be, of course, self-governed, as it will be their choice as well as duty to obey the laws.

It has been already remarked, that the refusal of a very small minority to obey will render force necessary. It has been also noted, that as every mass of people will inevitably desire a favorite, and fix their trust and affections upon one, it clearly follows that there will be of course a faction opposed to the public will as expressed in the laws. Now, if a faction is once admitted to exist in a state, the disposition and the means to obstruct the laws, or, in other words, the will of the majority, must be perceived to exist also. If then it be true, that a democratic government is of all the most liable to faction, which no man of sense will deny, it is manifest that it is, from its very nature, obliged more than any other government to resort to force to overcome or awe the power of faction. This latter will continually employ its own power, that acts always against the physical force of the nation, which can be brought to act only in extreme cases, and then, like every extreme remedy, aggravates the evil. For, let it be noted, a regular government, by overcoming an unsuccessful insurrection, becomes stronger; but elective rulers can scarcely ever employ the physical force of a democracy without turning the moral force, or the power of opinion, against the government. So that faction is not unfrequently made to triumph from its own defeats, and to avenge, in the dis-

grace and blood of magistrates, the crime of their fidelity to the laws.

As the boastful pretensions of the democratic system cannot be too minutely exposed, another consideration must be given to the subject.

That government certainly deserves no honest man's love or support, which, from the very laws of its being, carries terror and danger to the virtuous, and arms the vicious with authority and power. The essence, and in the opinion of many thousands not yet cured of their delusions, the excellence of democracy is, that it invests every citizen with an equal proportion of power. A state consisting of a million of citizens has a million sovereigns, each of whom detests all other sovereignty but his own. This very boast implies as much of the spirit of turbulence and insubordination as the utmost energy of any known regular government, even the most rigid, could keep in restraint. It also implies a state of agitation that is justly terrible to all who love their ease, and of instability that quenches the last hope of those who would transmit their liberty to posterity. Waiving any further pursuit of these reflections, let it be resumed, that if every man of the million has his ratable share of power in the community, then, instead of restraining the vicious, they also are armed with power, for they take their part; as they are citizens, this cannot be refused them. Now, as they have an interest in preventing the execution of the laws, which, in fact, is the apparent common interest of their whole class, their union will happen of course. The very first moment that they do unite, which it is ten thousand to one will happen before the form of the democracy is agreed upon, and while its plausible constitution is framing, that moment they form a faction, and the pretended efficacy of the democratic system, which is to operate by the power of opinion and persuasion, comes to an end. For an *imperium in imperio* exists; there is a state within the state, a combination interested and active in hindering the will of the majority from being obeyed. . . .

*   *   *

With the example of two rebellions against our revenue laws, it cannot be denied that our republic claims the submission, not merely of weak individuals, but of powerful combinations, of those whom distance, numbers, and enthusiasm embolden to deride its authority and defy its arms. A faction is a sort of empire within the empire, which acts by its own magistrates and laws, and prosecutes interests not only unlike, but destructive to those of the nation. The federalists are accused of attempting to impart too much energy to the administration, and of stripping, with too much severity, all such combinations of their assumed importance. Hence it is ridiculously absurd to denominate the federalists, the admirers and disciples of Washington, a faction.

But we shall be told, in defiance both of fact and good sense, that factions will not exist, or will be impotent if they do; for the majority have a right to govern, and certainly will govern by their representatives. Let their right be admitted, but they certainly will not govern in either of two cases, both fairly supposable, and likely, nay sure, to happen in succession: that a section of country, a combination, party, or faction, call it what you will, shall prove daring and potent enough to obstruct the laws and to exempt itself from their operation; or, growing bolder with impunity and success, finally by art, deceit, and perseverance, to force its chiefs into power, and thus, instead of submitting to the government, to bring the government into submission to a faction. Then the forms and the names of a republic will be used, and used more ostentatiously than ever; but its principles will be abused, and its ramparts and defences laid flat to the ground.

There are many, who, believing that a penful of ink can impart a deathless energy to a constitution, and having seen with pride and joy two or three skins of parchment added, like new walls about a fortress, to our own, will be filled with astonishment, and say, is

not our legislature divided? our executive single? our judiciary independent? Have we not amendments and bills of rights, excelling all compositions in prose? Where then can our danger lie? Our government, so we read, is constructed in such a manner as to defend itself and the people. We have the greatest political security, for we have adopted the soundest principles.—

To most grown children, therefore, the existence of faction will seem chimerical. Yet did any free state ever exist without the most painful and protracted conflicts with this foe? or expire any otherwise than by his triumph? The spring is not more genial to the grain and fruits, than to insects and vermin. The same sun that decks the fields with flowers, thaws out the serpent in the fen, and concocts his poison. Surely we are not the people to contest this position. Our present liberty was born into the world under the knife of this assassin, and now limps a cripple from his violence.

As soon as such a faction is known to subsist in force, we shall be told, the people may, and because they may they surely will, rally to discomfit and punish the conspirators. If the whole people in a body are to do this as often as it may be necessary, then it seems our political plan is to carry on our government by successive, or rather incessant revolutions. When the people deliberate and act in person, laying aside the plain truth, that it is impossible they should, all delegated authority is at an end; the representatives would be nothing in the presence of their assembled constituents. Thus falls or stops the machine of a regular government. Thus a faction, hostile to the government, would ensure their success by the very remedy that is supposed effectual to disappoint their designs. . . .

*   *   *

The people, it will be thought, will see their error and return. But there is no return to liberty. What the fire of faction does not destroy, it will debase. Those who have once tasted of the cup of sovereignty will be unfitted to be subjects; and those who have not, will scarcely form a wish, beyond the unmolested ignominy of slaves.

But will those who scorn to live at all unless they can live free, will these noble spirits abandon the public cause? Will they not break their chains on the heads of their oppressors? Suppose they attempt it, then we have a civil war; and when political diseases require the sword, the remedy will kill. Tyrants may be dethroned, and usurpers expelled and punished; but the sword, once drawn, cannot be sheathed. Whoever holds it, must rule by it; and that rule, though victory should give it to the best men and the honestest cause, cannot be liberty. Though painted as a goddess, she is mortal, and her spirit, once severed by the sword, can be evoked no more from the shades. . . .

*   *   *

If the positions laid down as theory could be denied, the brief history of the federal administration would establish them. It was first confided to the truest and purest patriot that ever lived. It succeeded a period, dismal and dark, and like the morning sun, lighted up a sudden splendor that was gratuitous, for it consumed nothing, but its genial rays cherished the powers of vegetation, while they displayed its exuberance. There was no example, scarcely a pretence of oppression; yet faction, basking in those rays, and sucking venom from the ground, even then cried out, "O sun, I tell thee, how I hate thy beams." Faction was organized sooner than the government.

If the most urgent public reasons could ever silence or satisfy the spirit of faction, the adoption of the new Constitution would have been prompt and unanimous. The government of a great nation had barely revenue enough to buy stationery for its clerks, or to pay the salary of the door-keeper. Public faith and public force were equally out of the question, for as it respected either authority or resources, the corporation of a college, or the missionary society were greater potentates than congress. Our federal government had not merely fallen into imbecility, and of course into contempt, but the oligarchical factions in the large states had actually made great advances in the usurpation of its powers. The king of New York levied imposts on Jersey and Connecticut; and the nobles of Virginia bore with impatience their tributary dependence on Baltimore and Philadelphia. Our discontents were fermenting into civil war; and that would have multiplied and exasperated our discontents.

Impending public evils, so obvious and so near, happily roused all the patriotism of the country; but they roused its ambition too. The great state chieftains found the sovereign power unoccupied, and . . . each employed intrigue, and would soon have employed force, to erect his province into a separate monarchy or aristocracy. Popular republican names would indeed have been used, but in the struggles of ambition, they would have been used only to cloak usurpation and tyranny. How late, and with what sourness and reluctance, did New York and Virginia renounce the hopes of aggrandizement which their antifederal leaders had so passionately cherished! The opposition to the adoption of the federal Constitution was not a controversy about principles; it was a struggle for power. In the great states, the ruling party, with that sagacity which too often accompanies inordinate ambition, instantly discerned, that if the new government should go into operation with all the energy that its letter and spirit would authorize, they must cease to rule—still worse, they must submit to be ruled, nay, worst of all, they must be ruled by their equals, a condition of real wretchedness and supposed disgrace, which our impatient tyrants anticipated with instinctive and unspeakable horror.

To prevent this dreaded result of the new Constitution, which, by securing a real legal equality to all the citizens, would bring them down to an equality, their earliest care was to bind the ties of their factious union more closely together; and by combining their influence and exerting the utmost malignity of their art, to render the new government odious and suspected by the people. Thus, conceived in jealousy and born in weakness and dissension, they hoped to see it sink, like its predecessor, the confederation, into contempt. Hence it was, that in every great state a faction arose with the fiercest hostility to the federal Constitution, and active in devising and pursuing every scheme, however unwarrantable or audacious, that would obstruct the establishment of any power in the state superior to its own.

It is undeniably true, therefore, that faction was organized sooner than the new government. We are not to charge this event to the accidental rivalships or disgusts of leading men, but to the operation of the invariable principles that preside over human actions and political affairs. Power had slipped out of the feeble hands of the old congress; and the world's power, like its wealth, can never lie one moment without a possessor. The states had instantly succeeded to the vacant sovereignty; and the leading men in the great states, for the small ones were inactive from a sense of their insignificance, engrossed their authority. Where the executive authority was single, the governor, as for instance in New York, felt his brow encircled with a diadem; but in those states where the governor is a mere cipher, the men who influenced the assembly governed the state, and there an oligarchy established itself. When has it been seen in the world, that the possession of sovereign power was regarded with indifference, or resigned without effort? If all that is ambition in the heart of man had slept in America, till the era of the new Constitution, the events of that period would not merely have awakened it into life, but have quickened it into all the agitations of frenzy.

Then commenced an active struggle for power. Faction resolved that the new government should not exist at all, or if that could not be prevented, that it should exist without energy. Accordingly, the presses of that time teemed with calumny and invective. Before the new government had done any thing, there was nothing oppressive or tyrannical which it was not accused of meditating; and when it began its operations, there was nothing wise or fit that it was not charged with neglecting; nothing right or beneficial that it did, but from an insidious design to delude and betray the people. The cry of usurpation and oppression was louder then, when all was prosperous and beneficent, than it has been since, when the judiciary is violently abolished, the judges dragged to the culprit's bar, the Constitution changed to prevent a change of rulers, and the path plainly marked out and already half travelled over, for the ambition of those rulers to reign in contempt of the people's votes, and on the ruins of their liberty.

He is certainly a political novice or a hypocrite, who will pretend that the antifederal opposition to the government is to be ascribed to the concern of the people for their liberties, rather than to the profligate ambition of their demagogues, eager for power, and suddenly alarmed by the imminent danger of losing it. . . . Their labor for twelve years was to inflame and deceive; and their recompense, for the last four, has been to degrade and betray.

Any person who considers the instability of all authority, that is not only derived from the multitude, but wanes or increases with the ever changing phases of their levity and caprice, will pronounce that the federal government was from the first, and from its very nature and organization, fated to sink under the rivalship of its state competitors for dominion. Virginia has never been more federal than it was, when, from considerations of policy, and perhaps in the hope of future success from its intrigues, it adopted the new Constitution; for it has never desisted from obstructing its measures, and urging every scheme that would reduce it back again to the imbecility of the old confederation. To the dismay of every true patriot, these arts have at length fatally succeeded; and our system of government now differs very little from what it would have been, if the impost proposed by the old congress had been granted, and the new federal Constitution had never been adopted by the States. In that case, the states being left to their natural inequality, the small states would have been, as they now are, nothing; and Virginia, potent in herself, more potent by her influence and intrigues, and uncontrolled by a superior federal head, would of course have been every thing. . . .

On evidence thus lamentably clear, I found my opinion, that the federalists can never again become the dominant party; in other words, the public reason and virtue cannot be again, as in our first twelve years, and never will be again the governing power, till our government has passed through its revolutionary changes. Every faction that may happen to rule will pursue but two objects, its vengeance on the fallen party, and the security of its own power against any new one that may rise to contest it. . . . Their objects are all selfish, all temporary. Mr. Jefferson's letters to Mazzei or Paine, his connection with Callender, or his mean condescensions to France and Spain, will add nothing to the weight of his disgrace with the party that shall supplant him. To be their enemy will be disgrace enough, and so far a refuge for his fame, as it will stop all curiosity and inquiry into particulars. . . .

The restoration of the federalists to their merited influence in the government supposes two things, the slumber or extinction of faction, and the efficacy of public morals. It supposes an interval of calm, when reason will dare to speak, and prejudice itself will incline to hear. Then, it is still hoped by many . . . the genuine public voice would call wisdom into power; and the love of country, which is the morality of politics, would guard and maintain its authority.

Are not these the visions that delight a poet's fancy, but will never revisit the statesman's eyes? When will faction sleep? Not till its labors of vengeance and ambition are over. Faction, we know, is the twin brother of our liberty,

and born first. . . . As long as there is a faction in full force, and possessed of the government, too, the public will and the public reason must have power to compel, as well as to convince, or they will convince without reforming. Bad men, whose rise by intrigue, may be dispossessed by worse men, who rise over their heads by deeper intrigue; but what has the public reason to do but to deplore its silence or to polish its chains? . . .

The public reason, therefore, is so little in a condition to reëstablish the federal cause, that it will not long maintain its own. Do we not see our giddy multitude celebrate with joy the triumphs of a party over some essential articles of our Constitution, and recently over one integral and independent branch of our government? . . . If federalism could by a miracle resume the reins of power, unless political virtue and pure morals should return also, those reins would soon drop or be snatched from its hands.

By political virtue is meant that love of country diffused through the society, and ardent in each individual, that would dispose, or rather impel every one to do or suffer much for his country, and permit no one to do any thing against it. . . .

Is there any resemblance in all this to the habits and passsions that predominate in America? Are not our people wholly engrossed by the pursuit of wealth and pleasure? Though grouped together into a society, the propensities of the individual still prevail; and if the nation discovers the rudiments of any character, they are yet to be developed. In forming it, have we not ground to fear that the sour, dissocial, malignant spirit of our politics will continue to find more to dread and hate in party, than to love and reverence in our country? What foundation can there be for that political virtue to rest upon, while the virtue of the society is proscribed, and its vice lays an exclusive claim to emolument and honor? And as long as faction governs, it must look to all that is vice in the state for its force, and to all that is virtue for its plunder. It is not merely the choice of faction, though no doubt base agents are to be preferred for base purposes, but it is its necessity also to keep men of true worth depressed by keeping the turbulent and worthless contented.

How then can love of country take root and grow in a soil, from which every valuable plant has thus been plucked up and thrown away as a weed? How can we forbear to identify the government with the country? and how is it possible that we should at the same time lavish all the ardor of our affection, and yet withhold every emotion either of confidence or esteem? It is said, that in republics majorities invariably oppress minorities. Can there be any real patriotism in a state which is thus filled with those who exercise and those who suffer tyranny? But how much less reason has any man to love that country, in which the voice of the majority is counterfeited, or the vicious, ignorant, and needy, are the instruments, and the wise and worthy are the victims of oppression?

When we talk of patriotism as the theme of declamation, it is not very material that we should know with any precision what we mean. It is a subject on which hypocrisy will seem to ignorance to be eloquent, because all of it will be received and well received as flattery. If, however, we search for a principle or sentiment general and powerful enough to produce national effects, capable of making a people act with constancy, or suffer with fortitude, is there any thing in our situation that could have produced, or that can cherish it? The straggling settlements of the southern part of the union, which now is the governing part, have been formed by emigrants from almost every nation of Europe. Safe in their solitudes, alike from the annoyance of enemies and of government, it is infinitely more probable that they will sink into barbarism than rise to the dignity of national sentiment and character. Patriotism, to be a powerful or steady principle of action, must be deeply imbued by education, and strongly impressed both by the policy of the government and the

course of events. To love our country with ardor, we must often have some fears for its safety; our affection will be exalted in its distress; and our self-esteem will glow on the contemplation of its glory. It is only by such diversified and incessant exercise that the sentiment can become strong in the individual, or be diffused over the nation.

But how can that nation have any such affinities, any sense of patriotism, whose capacious wilderness receives and separates from each other the successive troops of emigrants from all other nations, men who remain ignorant, or learn only from the newspapers that they are countrymen, who think it their right to be exempted from all tax, restraint, or control, and of course that they have nothing to do with or for their country, but to make rulers for it, who, after they are made, are to have nothing to do with their makers; a country, too, which they are sure will not be invaded, and cannot be enslaved? . . . It is difficult to conceive of a country, which, from the manner of its settlement, or the manifest tendencies of its politics, is more destitute or more incapable of being inspired with political virtue.

What foundation remains, then, for the hopes of those who expect to see the federalists again invested with power?

Shall we be told, that if the nation is not animated with public spirit, the individuals are at least fitted to be good citizens by the purity of their morals? But what are morals without restraints? and how will merely voluntary restraints be maintained? How long will sovereigns, as the people are made to fancy they are, insist more upon checks than prerogatives? . . .

Besides, in political reasoning it is generally overlooked, that if the existence of morals should encourage a people to prefer a democratic system, the operation of that system is sure to destroy their morals. Power in such a society cannot long have any regular control; and, without control, it is itself a vice. Is there in human affairs an occasion of profligacy more shameless or more contagious than a general election? Every spring gives birth and gives wings to this epidemic mischief. Then begins a sort of tillage, that turns up to the sun and air the most noxious weeds in the kindliest soil; or, to speak still more seriously, it is a mortal pestilence, that begins with rottenness in the marrow. A democratic society will soon find its morals the encumbrance of its race, the surly companion of its licentious joys. It will encourage its demagogues to impeach and persecute the magistracy, till it is no longer disquieted. In a word, there will not be morals without justice; and though justice might possibly support a democracy, yet a democracy cannot possibly support justice. . . .

Federalism was therefore manifestly founded on a mistake, on the supposed existence of sufficient political virtue, and on the permanency and authority of the public morals.

The party now in power committed no such mistake. They acted on the knowledge of what men actually are, not what they ought to be. Instead of enlightening the popular understanding, their business was to bewilder it. They knew that the vicious, on whom society makes war, would join them in their attack upon government. They inflamed the ignorant; they flattered the vain; they offered novelty to the restless; and promised plunder to the base. The envious were assured that the great should fall; and the ambitious that *they* should become great. The federal power, propped by nothing but opinion, fell, not because it deserved its fall, but because its principles of action were more exalted and pure than the people could support.

It is now undeniable that the federal administration was blameless. It has stood the scrutiny of time, and passed unharmed through the ordeal of its enemies. With all the evidence of its conduct in their possession, and with servile majorities at their command, it has not been in their power, much as they desired it, to fix any reproach on their predecessors.

It is the opinion of a few, but a very groundless opinion, that the cause of order will be reëstablished by the splitting of the reigning jacobins; or, if that should not take place soon, the union will be divided, and the northern confederacy compelled to provide for its own liberty. Why, it is said, should we expect that the union of the bad will be perfect, when that of the Washington party, though liberty and property were at stake, has been broken? And why should it be supposed that the Northern States, who possess so prodigious a preponderance of white population, of industry, commerce, and civilization over the Southern, will remain subject to Virginia? Popular delusion cannot last, and as soon as the opposition of the federalists ceases to be feared, the conquerors will divide into new factions, and either the federalists will be called again into power, or the union will be severed into two empires. . . .

As there is nothing really excellent in our governments, that is not novel in point of institution, and which faction has not represented as old in abuse, the natural vanity, presumption, and restlessness of the human heart have, from the first, afforded the strength of a host to the jacobins of our country. The ambitious desperadoes are the natural leaders of this host.

Now, though such leaders may have many occasions of jealousy and discord with one another, especially in the division of power and booty, is it not absurd to suppose, that any set of them will endeavor to restore both to the right owners? Do we expect a self-denying ordinance from the sons of violence and rapine? Are not those remarkably inconsistent with themselves, who say, our republican system is a government of justice and order, that was freely adopted in peace, subsists by morals, and whose office it is to ask counsel of the wise and to give protection to the good, yet who console themselves in the storms of the state with the fond hope that order will spring out of confusion, because innovators will grow weary of change, and the ambitious will contend about their spoil. Then we are to have a new system exactly like the old one, from the fortuitous concourse of atoms, from the crash and jumble of all that is precious or sacred in the state. It is said, the popular hopes and fears are the gales that impel the political vessel. Can any disappointment of such hopes be greater than their folly?

It is true, the men now in power may not be united together by patriotism, or by any principle of faith or integrity. It is also true, that they have not, and cannot easily have, a military force to awe the people into submission. But on the other hand, they have no need of an army; there is no army to oppose them. They are held together by the ties, and made irresistible by the influence of party. With the advantage of acting as the government, who can oppose them? Not the federalists, who neither have any force, nor any object to employ it for, if they had. Not any subdivision of their own faction, because the opposers, if they prevail, will become the government, so much the less liable to be opposed for their recent victory; and if the new sect should fail, they will be nothing. The conquerors will take care that an unsuccessful resistance shall strengthen their domination.

Thus it seems, in every event of the division of the ruling party, the friends of true liberty have nothing to hope. Tyrants may thus be often changed, but the tyranny will remain.

A democracy cannot last. Its nature ordains, that its next change shall be into a military despotism, of all known governments, perhaps, the most prone to shift its head, and the slowest to mend its vices. The reason is, that the tyranny of what is called the people, and that by the sword, both operate alike to debase and corrupt, till there are neither men left with the spirit to desire liberty, nor morals with the power to sustain justice. Like the burning pestilence that destroys the human body, nothing can subsist by its dissolution but vermin.

A military government may make a nation great, but it cannot make them free. There will be frequent and bloody struggles to decide who shall hold the sword; but the conqueror will destroy his competitors and prevent any permanent division of the empire. Experience proves, that in all such governments

there is a continual tendency to unity....

* * *

The jacobins are indeed ignorant or wicked enough to say, a mixed monarchy, on the model of the British, will succeed the failure of our republican system. Mr. Jefferson in his famous letter to Mazzei has shown the strange condition both of his head and heart, by charging this design upon Washington and his adherents. It is but candid to admit, that there are many weak-minded democrats who really think a mixed monarchy the next stage of our politics. As well might they promise, that when their factious fire has burned the plain dwelling-house of our liberty, her temple will rise in royal magnificence, and with all the proportions of Grecian architecture, from the ashes. It is impossible sufficiently to elucidate, yet one could never be tired of elucidating the matchless absurdity of this opinion....

* * *

Is our monarchy to be supported by the national habits of subordination and implicit obedience? Surely when they hold out this expectation, the jacobins do not mean to answer for themselves. Or do we really think it would still be a monarchy, though we should set up, and put down at pleasure, a town-meeting king?...

Now is there one of those essential principles, that it is even possible for the American people to adopt for their monarchy? Are old habits to be changed by a vote, and new ones to be established without experience? Can we have a monarchy without a peerage? or shall our governors supply that defect by giving commissions to a sufficient number of nobles of the quorum? Where is the American hierarchy?...

It is not recollected that any monarchy in the world was ever introduced by consent; nor will any one believe, on reflection, that it could be maintained by any nation, if nothing but consent upheld it. It is a rare thing for a people to choose their government; it is beyond all credibility, that they will enjoy the still rarer opportunity of changing it by choice.

The notion, therefore, of an American mixed monarchy is supremely ridiculous. It is highly probable our country will be eventually subject to a monarchy, but it is demonstrable that it cannot be such as the British; and whatever it may be, that the votes of the citizens will not be taken to introduce it.

It cannot be expected that the tendency towards a change of government, however obvious, will be discerned by the multitude of our citizens. While demagogues enjoy their favor, their passions will have no rest, and their judgment and understanding no exercise. Otherwise it might be of use to remind them, that more essential breaches have been made in our constitution within four years than in the British in the last hundred and forty. . . .

Let every citizen who is able to think, and who can bear the pain of thinking, make the contrast at his leisure.

They are certainly blind who do not see that we are descending from a supposed orderly and stable republican government into a licentious democracy, with a progress that baffles all means to resist, and scarcely leaves leisure to deplore its celerity. The institutions and the hopes that Washington raised are nearly prostrate; and his name and memory would perish, if the rage of his enemies had any power over history. But they have not—history will give scope to her vengeance, and posterity will not be defrauded.

But if our experience had not clearly given warning of our approaching catastrophe, the very nature of democracy would inevitably produce it.

A government by the passions of the multitude, or, no less correctly, according to the vices and ambition of their leaders, is a democracy. We have heard so long of the indefeasible sovereignty of the people, and have admitted so many specious theories of the rights of man, which are contradicted by his na-

ture and experience, that few will dread at all, and fewer still will dread as they ought, the evils of an American democracy. They will not believe them near, or they will think them tolerable or temporary. Fatal delusion!

When it is said, there may be a tyranny of the *many* as well as of the *few*, every democrat will yield at least a cold and speculative assent; but he will at all times act, as if it were a thing incomprehensible, that there should be any evil to be apprehended in the uncontrolled power of the people. He will say arbitrary power may make a tyrant, but how can it make its possessor a slave?

In the first place, let it be remarked, the power of individuals is a very different thing from their liberty. When I vote for the man I prefer, he may happen not to be chosen; or he may disappoint my expectations if he is; or he may be outvoted by others in the public body to which he is elected. I may then hold and exercise all the power that a citizen can have or enjoy, and yet such laws may be made and such abuses allowed as shall deprive me of all liberty. I may be tried by a jury, and that jury may be culled and picked out from my political enemies by a federal marshal. Of course, my life and liberty may depend on the good pleasure of the man who appoints that marshal. I may be assessed arbitrarily for my faculty, or upon conjectural estimation of my property, so that all I have shall be at the control of the government, whenever its displeasure shall exact the sacrifice. I may be told that I am a federalist, and as such bound to submit, in all cases whatsoever, to the will of the majority, as the ruling faction ever pretend to be. My submission may be tested by my resisting or obeying commands that will involve me in disgrace, or drive me to despair. I may become a fugitive, because the ruling party have made me afraid to stay at home; or, perhaps, while I remain at home, they may, nevertheless, think fit to inscribe my name on the list of emigrants and proscribed persons.

All this was done in France, and many of the admirers of French examples are impatient to imitate them. All this time the people may be told, they are the freest in the world; but what ought my opinion to be? What would the threatened clergy, the aristocracy of wealthy merchants, as they have been called already, and thirty thousand more in Massachusetts, who vote for Governor Strong, and whose case might be no better than mine, what would they think of their condition? Would they call it liberty? Surely, here is oppression sufficient in extent and degree to make the government that inflicts it both odious and terrible; yet this and a thousand times more than this was practised in France, and will be repeated as often as it shall please God in his wrath to deliver a people to the dominion of their licentious passions.

The people, as a body, cannot deliberate. Nevertheless, they will feel an irresistible impulse to act, and their resolutions will be dictated to them by their demagogues. The consciousness, or the opinion, that they possess the supreme power, will inspire inordinate passions; and the violent men, who are the most forward to gratify those passions, will be their favorites. What is called the government of the people is in fact too often the arbitrary power of such men. Here, then, we have the faithful portrait of democracy. What avails the boasted power of individual citizens? or of what value is the will of the majority, if that will is dictated by a committee of demagogues, and law and right are in fact at the mercy of a victorious faction? To make a nation free, the crafty must be kept in awe, and the violent in restraint. The weak and the simple find their liberty arise not from their own individual sovereignty, but from the power of law and justice over all. It is only by the due restraint of others, that I am free.

Popular sovereignty is scarcely less beneficent than awful, when it resides in their courts of justice; there its office, like a sort of human providence, is to warn, enlighten, and protect; when the people are inflamed to seize and exercise it in their assemblies, it is competent only to kill and destroy. Temperate liberty is like the dew, as it falls unseen from its own heaven; constant without excess, it finds vegetation thirsting for its refreshment, and imparts to it the vigor to take more. All nature, moistened with blessings, sparkles in the morning ray. But democracy is a water-spout that bursts from the clouds, and lays the ravaged earth bare to its rocky foundations. The labors of man lie whelmed with his hopes beneath masses of ruin, that bury not only the dead but their monuments.

It is the almost universal mistake of our countrymen, that democracy would be mild and safe in America. They charge the horrid excesses of France not so much to human nature, which will never act better, when the restraints of government, morals, and religion are thrown off, but to the characteristic cruelty and wickedness of Frenchmen.

The truth is, and let it humble our pride, the most ferocious of all animals, when his passions are roused to fury and are uncontrolled, is man; and of all governments, the worst is that which never fails to excite, but was never found to restrain those passions, that is, democracy. It is an illuminated hell, that in the midst of remorse, horror, and torture, rings with festivity; for experience shows, that one joy remains to this most malignant description of the damned, the power to make others wretched. When a man looks round and sees his neighbors mild and merciful, he cannot feel afraid of the abuse of their power over him; and surely if they oppress me, he will say, they will spare their own liberty, for that is dear to all mankind. It is so. The human heart is so constituted, that a man loves liberty as naturally as himself. Yet liberty is a rare thing in the world, though the love of it is so universal. . . .

The nature of arbitrary power is always odious; but it cannot be long the arbitrary power of the multitude. There is, probably, no form of rule among mankind, in which the progress of the government depends so little on the particular character of those who administer it. Democracy is the creature of impulse and violence; and the intermediate stages towards the tyranny of one are so quickly passed, that the vileness and cruelty of men are displayed with surprising uniformity. There is not time for great talents to act. There is no sufficient reason to believe, that we should conduct a revolution with much more mildness than the French. If a revolution find the citizens lambs, it will soon make them carnivorous, if not cannibals. . . . There is no governing power in the state but party. The moderate and thinking part of the citizens are without power or influence; and it must be so, because all power and influence are engrossed by a factious combination of men, who can overwhelm uncombined individuals with numbers, and the wise and virtuous with clamor and fury.

It is indeed a law of politics, as well as of physics, that a body in action must overcome an equal body at rest. The attacks that have been made on the constitutional barriers proclaim, in a tone that would not be louder from a trumpet, that party will not tolerate any resistance to its will. All the supposed independent orders of the commonwealth must be its servile instruments, or its victims. We should experience the same despotism in Massachusetts, New Hampshire, and Connecticut, but the battle is not yet won. It will be won; and they who already display the temper of their Southern and French allies, will not linger or reluct in imitating the worst extremes of their example.

What, then, is to be our condition?

Faction will inevitably triumph. Where the government is both stable and free, there may be parties. There will be differences of opinion, and the pride of opinion will be sufficient to generate contests, and to inflame them with bitterness and rancor. There will be rivalships among those whom genius, fame, or station have made great, and these will deeply agitate the state without often hazarding its safety. Such parties will excite alarm, but they may be safely left, like the elements, to exhaust their fury upon each other.

The object of their strife is to get power *under* the government; for, where

that is constituted as it should be, the power *over* the government will not seem attainable, and, of course, will not be attempted.

But in democratic states there will be factions. The sovereign power being nominally in the hands of all, will be effectively within the grasp of a few; and therefore, by the very laws of our nature, a few will combine, intrigue, lie, and fight to engross it to themselves. All history bears testimony, that this attempt has never yet been disappointed.

Who will be the associates? Certainly not the virtuous, who do not wish to control the society, but quietly to enjoy its protection. The enterprising merchant, the thriving tradesman, the careful farmer, will be engrossed by the toils of their business, and will have little time or inclination for the unprofitable and disquieting pursuits of politics. It is not the industrious, sober husbandman, who will plough that barren field; it is the lazy and dissolute bankrupt, who has no other to plough. The idle, the ambitious, and the needy will band together to break the hold that law has upon them, and then to get hold of law. Faction is a Hercules, whose first labor is to strangle this lion, and then to make armor of his skin. In every democratic state, the ruling faction will have law to keep down its enemies; but it will arrogate to itself an undisputed power over law. If our ruling faction has found any impediments, we ask, which of them is now remaining? And is it not absurd to suppose, that the conquerors will be contented with half the fruits of victory?

We are to be subject, then, to a despotic faction, irritated by the resistance that has delayed, and the scorn that pursues their triumph, elate with the insolence of an arbitrary and uncontrollable domination, and who will exercise their sway, not according to the rules of integrity or national policy, but in conformity with their own exclusive interests and passions.

This is a state of things which admits of progress, but not of reformation; it is the beginning of a revolution, which must advance. Our affairs, as first observed, no longer depend on counsel.

The opinion of a majority is no longer invited or permitted to control our destinies, or even to retard their consummation. The men in power may, and no doubt will give place to some other faction, who will succeed, because they are abler men, or possibly, in candor we say it, because they are worse. Intrigue will for some time answer instead of force, or the mob will supply it. But by degrees force only will be relied on by those who are *in*, and employed by those who are *out*. The vis major will prevail, and some bold chieftain will conquer liberty, and triumph and reign in her name.

Yet it is confessed, we have hopes that this event is not very near. We have no cities as large as London or Paris; and of course the ambitious demagogues may find the ranks of their standing army too thin to rule by them alone. It is also worth remark, that our mobs are not, like those of Europe, excitable by the cry of no bread. The dread of famine is everywhere else a power of political electricity, that glides through all the haunts of filth, and vice, and want in a city, with incredible speed, and in times of insurrection rives and scorches with a sudden force, like heaven's own thunder. Accordingly, we find the sober men of Europe more afraid of the despotism of the rabble than of the government.

But as in the United States we see less of this description of low vulgar, and as in the essential circumstance alluded to, they are so much less manageable by their demagogues, we are to expect that our affairs will be long guided by courting the mob, before they are violently changed by employing them. While the passions of the multitude can be conciliated to confer power and to overcome all impediments to its action, our rulers have a plain and easy task to perform. It costs them nothing but hypocrisy. As soon, however, as rival favorites of the people may happen to contend by the practice of the same arts, we are to look for the sanguinary strife of ambition. . . . The revolution will proceed in exactly the same way, but not with so rapid a pace, as that of France.

Mercy Otis Warren

A FAVORABLE VIEW OF WASHINGTON

Mercy Otis Warren (1728–1814), an outspoken Jeffersonian Republican, partisan historian, and wife of one of Massachusetts' leading
politicians, viewed the Federalist party as a many-headed monster that
threatened the liberties of the people. A participant in the factional fights
within her native state, she portrayed the 1790's as an age of raging
political passions. But her view of Washington was at variance with the
rest of her thesis. She saw Washington as an Olympian figure who was
above petty politics, and his Farewell Address as a public-spirited exhor-
tation to the people. In her eyes, John Adams represented the typical
Federalist: he was unprincipled, vindictive, and, worst of all, a monarchist.

PREVIOUS to general Washington's
second return to his rural amuse-
ments, he published a farewell address
to the inhabitants of the United States,
fraught with advice worthy of the statesman, the hero, and the citizen. He exhorted them to union among themselves, economy in public expenditure,
sobriety, temperance, and industry in
private life. He solemnly warned them
against the danger of foreign influence,
exhorted them to observe good faith and
justice toward all nations, to cultivate
peace and harmony with all, to indulge
no inveterate antipathies against any,
or passionate attachments for particular
nations, but to be constantly awake
against the insidious wiles of foreign
influence, observing, that "this was one
of the most baneful foes of republican
government." This was indeed, after
they were split into factions; after an
exotic taste had been introduced into
America, which had a tendency to en-
hance their public and to accumulate
their private debts; and after the poison
of foreign influence had crept into their
councils, and created a passion to as-
similate the politics and the government
of the United States nearer to the model
of European monarchies than the letter
of the constitution, by any fair construction, would admit. It was also, after lux-
ury had spread over every class, while
the *stimulus* to private industry was in
a degree cut off by the capture of their
shipping by the belligerent powers, under various pretences of the breach of
neutrality.

After this period new contingencies
arose, and new discussions were required with regard to foreign relations
and connexions, that had no pacific
operation, or any tendency to conciliate
the minds, or to quiet the perturbed
spirits of existing parties.

The operations and the consequences
of the civil administration of the first
president of the United States, notwithstanding the many excellent qualities
of his heart, and the virtues which
adorned his life, have since been viewed
at such opposite points, that further
strictures on his character and conduct
shall be left to future historians, after
time has mollified the passions and prejudices of the present generation. A new
constitution, and an extensive government, in which he acted eight years as
chief magistrate, open a new field of
observation, for future pens to descant
on the merits or demerits of a man, admired abroad, beloved at home, and celebrated through half the globe: this will
be done according to the variety of
opinions which will ever exist among
mankind, when character is surveyed in
the cool moments of calm philosophy,

From Mercy Otis Warren, *History of the Rise, Progress and Termination of the American Revolution etc.* (3 vols., Boston, 1805), Vol. III, pp. 388–391, 392–395.

which contemplates the nature and passions of man, and the contingent circumstances, that lift him to the skies, or leave him in the shade of doubtful opinion.

Public opinion is generally grounded on truth; but the enthusiasm to which the greatest part of mankind are liable, often urges the passions to such a degree of extravagance, as to confound the just ratio of praise or reproach: but the services and merits of general Washington, are so deeply engraven on the hearts of his countrymen, that no time or circumstance will or ought ever to efface the lustre of his well earned reputation.

We have already seen, that after the peace, the infant confederated states exhibited scenes and disclosed projects that open too wide a field for discussion, to bring down a regular historical work, farther than the moment which winds up the drama of the military, political, and civil administration of a man, whose name will have a conspicuous place in all future historical records.

History may not furnish an example of a person so generally admired, and possessed of equal opportunities for making himself the despotic master of the liberties of his country, who had the moderation repeatedly to divest himself of all authority, and retire to private life with the sentiments expressed by himself in the close of his farewell address: he there observed—"I anticipate with pleasing expectation that retreat, in which I promise myself to realize, without alloy, the sweet enjoyment of partaking, in the midst of my fellow citizens, the benign influence of good laws under a free government—the ever favorite object of my heart, and the happy reward, as I trust, of our mutual cares, labors, and dangers."

The commander of the armies of the United States, has been conducted from the field of war, and from the zenith of civil command, to the delicious retreats of peaceful solitude. We now leave him in the shade of retirement, with fervent wishes that he may wind up the career of human life in that tranquillity which becomes the hero and the Christian.

*   *   *

Mr. Adams was undoubtedly a statesman of penetration and ability; but his prejudices and his passions were sometimes too strong for his sagacity and judgment.

After Great Britain had acknowledged the independence of the dismembered colonies, Mr. Adams was sent to England, with a view of negociating a treaty of commerce; but the government too sore from the loss of the colonies, and the nation too much soured by the breach, nothing was done. He however resided there four or five years; and unfortunately for himself and his country, he became so enamoured with the British constitution, and the government, manners, and laws of the nation, that a partiality for monarchy appeared, which was inconsistent with his former professions of republicanism. Time and circumstances often lead so imperfect a creature as man to view the same thing in a very different point of light.

After Mr. Adams's return from England, he was implicated by a large portion of his countrymen, as having relinquished the republican system, and forgotten the principles of the American revolution, which he had advocated for near twenty years.

The political errors of men of talents, sometimes spring from their own passions; often from their prejudices imbibed by local or incidental circumstances; and not unfrequently from the versatile condition of man, which renders it difficult, at one period, to decide on the best system of civil government; or at another, on the most effectual means of promoting the general happiness of mankind. This may lead the candid mind to cast a veil over that ambiguity which confounds opinion, and that counteraction of former principles, which often sets a man in opposition to himself, and prevents that uniformity of conduct which dignifies, and that consistency which adorns the character.

Pride of talents and much ambition, were undoubtedly combined in the character of the president who immediately succeeded general Washington, and the existing circumstances of his country, with his own capacity for business, gave him an opportunity for the full gratification of the most prominent features of his character.

Endowed with a comprehensive genius, well acquainted with the history of men and of nations; and having long appeared to be actuated by the principles of integrity, by a zeal for the rights of men, and an honest indignation at the ideas of despotism, it was viewed as a kind of political phenomenon, when discovered that Mr. Adams's former opinions were beclouded by a partiality for monarchy. It may however be charitably presumed, that by living long near the splendor of courts and courtiers, with other concurring circumstances, he might become so biassed in his judgment as to think that an hereditary monarchy was the best government for his native country. From his knowledge of men, he was sensible it was easy to turn the tide of public opinion in favor of any system supported by plausible argumentation. Thus he drew a doleful picture of the confusion and dissolution of all republics, and presented it to the eyes of his countrymen, under the title of a "Defence of their constitutions." This had a powerful tendency to shake the republican system through the United States. Yet the predilection of Americans in general, in favor of a republican form of government was so strong, that few had the hardiness to counteract it, until several years after the United States had come an independent nation.

On Mr. Adams's return from England, he undoubtedly discovered a partiality in favor of monarchic government, and few scrupled to assert for a time, that he exerted his abilities to encourage the operation of those principles in America. But any further strictures are unnecessary in this place on the character of a gentleman, whose official stations, abilities and services, amidst the revolutionary conflict, may probably excite some future historian to investigate the causes of his lapse from former republican principles, and to observe with due propriety on his administration and its consequences while president of the United States.

James Madison

AN UNFAVORABLE VIEW OF WASHINGTON'S SUPPORTERS

James Madison, reputed by many historians to be the mastermind behind the formation of the Republican party, gives evidence below of the vituperation that colored the politics of the period. To Madison the men in the government during Washington's first administration could be broken down into two groups—the "Anti-republicans" and the "Republicans." The "Anti-republicans," or Federalist prototypes, were without ideals and scruples; their sole goal was to serve their own interests. The "Republicans," on the other hand, were the "best keepers of the people's liberties," because they were ready to base the government upon the will of the people. Madison's piece and the selections by Hamilton in this book reflect the two prevailing political philosophies of the time. The "Republican" view here presents the Lockeian proposition that the original state of nature was good and that men were equal and independent; the other, the Hobbesian position, that men in their natural state are self-seeking, brutish, and constantly warring upon one another.

WHO ARE THE BEST KEEPERS OF THE PEOPLE'S LIBERTIES?

Republican.—The people themselves. —The sacred trust can be no where so safe as in the hands most interested in preserving it.

Anti-republican.—The people are stupid, suspicious, licentious. They cannot safely trust themselves. When they have established government they should think of nothing but obedience, leaving the care of their liberties to their wiser rulers.

Republican.—Although all men are born free, and all nations might be so, yet too true it is, that slavery has been the general lot of the human race. Ignorant—they have been cheated; asleep —they have been surprized; divided— the yoke has been forced upon them. But what is the lesson? that because the people *may* betray themselves, they ought to give themselves up, blindfold, to those who have an interest in betraying them? Rather conclude that the people ought to be enlightened, to be awakened, to be united, that after establishing a government they should watch over it, as well as obey it.

Anti-republican.—You look at the surface only, where errors float, instead of fathoming the depths where truth lies hid. It is not the government that is disposed to fly off from the people; but the people that are ever ready to fly off from the government. Rather say then, enlighten the government, warn it to be vigilant, enrich it with influence, arm it with force, and to the people never pronounce but two words—*Submission* and *Confidence.*

Republican.—The centrifugal tendency then is in the people, not in the government, and the secret art lies in restraining the tendency, by augmenting the attractive principle of the government with all the weight that can be added to it. What a perversion of the natural order of things! to make *power* the primary and central object of the social system, and *Liberty* but its satellite.

Anti-republican.—The science of the stars can never instruct you in the mysteries of government. Wonderful as it may seem, the more you increase the attractive force of power, the more you enlarge the sphere of liberty; the more

From Gaillard Hunt, ed., *The Writings of James Madison* (New York, 1906), Vol. VI, pp. 120–123.

you make government independent and hostile towards the people, the better security you provide for their rights and interests. Hence the wisdom of the theory, which, after limiting the share of the people to a third of the government, and lessening the influence of that share by the mode and term of delegating it, establishes two grand hereditary orders, with feelings, habits, interests, and prerogatives all inveterately hostile to the rights and interests of the people, yet by a *mysterious* operation all combining to fortify the people in both.

Republican.—Mysterious indeed!— But mysteries belong to religion, not to government; to the ways of the Almighty, not to the works of man. And in religion itself there is nothing mysteri- ous to its author; the mystery lies in the dimness of the human sight. So in the institutions of man let there be no mystery, unless for those inferior beings endowed with a ray perhaps of the twilight vouchsafed to the first order of terrestrial creation.

Anti-republican.—You are destitute, I perceive, of every quality of good citizen, or rather of a good *subject*. You have neither the light of faith nor the spirit of obedience. I denounce you to the government as an accomplice of atheism and anarchy.

Republican.—And I forbear to denounce you to the people, though a blasphemer of their rights and an idolater of tyranny.—Liberty disdains to persecute.

James Madison

A CANDID STATEMENT ON PARTIES

Madison, writing an essay in 1792 on America's political parties, raised the question as to who was better equipped to rule the country—the elite, or the plain people? The "Anti-republicans" being more partial to the wealthy upper class and hoping to retain power in the hands of the few, believed that ordinary men were incapable of governing themselves, according to Madison. The "Republicans"—with whom Madison identified himself—hated the idea of hereditary power, and held that the mass of people could recognize the public good and could be counted upon to act in accordance with that principle.

As it is the business of the contemplative statesman to trace the history of parties in a free country, so it is the duty of the citizen at all times to understand the actual state of them. Whenever this duty is omitted, an opportunity is given to designing men, by the use of artificial or nominal distinctions, to oppose and balance against each other those who never differed as to the end to be pursued, and may no longer differ as to the means of attaining it. The most interesting state of parties in the United States may be referred to three periods: Those who espoused the cause of independence and those who adhered to the British claims, formed the parties of the first period; if, indeed, the disaffected class were considerable enough to deserve the name of a party. This state of things was superseded by the treaty of peace in 1783. From 1783 to 1787 there were parties in abundance, but being rather local than general, they are not within the present review.

The Federal Constitution, proposed in the latter year, gave birth to a second and most interesting division of the people. Every one remembers it, because every one was involved in it.

Among those who embraced the constitution, the great body were unquestionably friends to republican liberty; tho' there were, no doubt, some who were openly or secretly attached to monarchy and aristocracy; and hoped to make the constitution a cradle for these hereditary establishments.

Among those who opposed the constitution, the great body were certainly well affected to the union and to good government, tho' there might be a few who had a learning unfavourable to both. This state of parties was terminated by the regular and effectual establishment of the federal government in 1788; out of the administration of which, however, has arisen a third division, which being natural to most political societies, is likely to be of some duration in ours.

One of the divisions consists of those, who from particular interest, from natural temper, or from the habits of life, are more partial to the opulent than to the other classes of society; and having debauched themselves into a persuasion that mankind are incapable of governing themselves, it follows with them, of course, that government can be carried on only by the pageantry of rank, the influence of money and emoluments, and the terror of military force. Men of those sentiments must naturally wish to point the measures of government less to the interest of the many than of a few, and less to the reason of the many than to their weaknesses; hoping perhaps in proportion to the ardor of their zeal, that by giving such a turn to the administration, the government

From Gaillard Hunt, ed., *The Writings of James Madison* (New York, 1906), Vol. VI, pp. 106–119.

itself may by degrees be narrowed into fewer hands, and approximated to an hereditary form.

The other division consists of those who believing in the doctrine that mankind are capable of governing themselves, and hating hereditary power as an insult to the reason and an outrage to the rights of man, are naturally offended at every public measure that does not appeal to the understanding and to the general interest of the community, or that is not strictly conformable to the principles, and conducive to the preservation of republican government.

This being the real state of parties among us, an experienced and dispassionate observer will be at no loss to decide on the probable conduct of each.

The anti republican party, as it may be called, being the weaker in point of numbers, will be induced by the most obvious motives to strengthen themselves with the men of influence, particularly of moneyed, which is the most active and insinuating influence. It will be equally their true policy to weaken their opponents by reviving exploded parties, and taking advantage of all prejudices, local, political, and occupational, that may prevent or disturb a general coalition of sentiments.

The republican party, as it may be termed, conscious that the mass of people in every part of the union, in every state, and of every occupation must at bottom be with them, both in interest and sentiment, will naturally find their account in burying all antecedent questions, in banishing every other distinction than that between enemies and friends to republican government, and in promoting a general harmony among the latter, wherever residing, or however employed.

Whether the republican or the rival party will ultimately establish its ascendance, is a problem which may be contemplated now; but which time alone can solve. On one hand experience shews that in politics as in war, stratagem is often an overmatch for numbers; and among more happy characteristics of our political situation, it is now well understood that there are peculiarities, some temporary, others more durable, which may favour that side in the contest. On the republican side, again, the superiority of numbers is so great, their sentiments are so decided, and the practice of making a common cause, where there is a common sentiment and common interest, in spight of circumstantial and artificial distinctions, is so well understood, that no temperate observer of human affairs will be surprised if the issue in the present instance should be reversed, and the government be administered in the spirit and form approved by the great body of the people.

Thomas Jefferson

UNPOPULAR POLICIES, MID-1790's

Thomas Jefferson is often pictured as a dreamy-eyed idealist: the chief spokesman for those who wanted to make America an agrarian commonwealth based upon the virtues of sturdy, independent yeoman-farmers. The two selections that follow reveal another side of Jefferson—the practical politician. In the first selection below, Jefferson displays his political acumen by predicting the defeat of the "Anti-republicans," or Federalists, as early as 1795. The Federalists, claimed Jefferson, were bound to lose in time because their policies were unpopular with the mass of people.

THE people of America, before the revolution-war, being attached to England, had taken up, without examination, the English ideas of the superiority of their constitution over every thing of the kind which ever had been or ever would be tried. The revolution forced them to consider the subject for themselves, and the result was an universal conversion to republicanism. Those who did not come over to this opinion, either left us, & were called Refugees, or staid with us under the name of tories; & some, preferring profit to principle took side with us and floated with the general tide. Our first federal constitution, or confederation as it was called, was framed in the first moments of our separation from England, in the highest point of our jealousies of independance as to her & as to each other. It formed therefore too weak a bond to produce an union of action as to foreign nations. This appeared at once on the establishment of peace, when the pressure of a common enemy which had hooped us together during the war, was taken away. Congress was found to be quite unable to point the action of the several states to a common object. A general desire therefore took place of amending the federal constitution. This was opposed by some of those who wished for monarchy to wit, the Refugees now returned, the old tories, & the timid whigs who prefer tranquility to freedom, hoping monarchy might be the remedy if a state of complete anarchy could be brought on. A Convention however being decided on, some of the monocrats got elected, with a hope of introducing an English constitution, when they found that the great body of the delegates were strongly for adhering to republicanism, & for giving due strength to their government under that form, they then directed their efforts to the assimilation of all the parts of the new government to the English constitution as nearly as was attainable. In this they were not altogether without success; insomuch that the monarchical features of the new constitution produced a violent opposition to it from the most zealous republicans in the several states. For this reason, & because they also thought it carried the principle of a consolidation of the states farther than was requisite for the purpose of producing an union of action as to foreign powers, it is still doubted by some whether a majority of the people of the U.S. were not against adopting it. However it was carried through all the assemblies of the states, tho' by very small majorities in the largest states. The inconveniences of an inefficient government, driving the people as is usual, into the opposite extreme, the elections to the first Congress run very much in favor of those who were known to favor a very strong government. Hence the

From Paul Leicester Ford, ed., *The Works of Thomas Jefferson* (New York, 1904), Vol. VIII, pp. 206–210.

anti-republicans appeared a considerable majority in both houses of Congress. They pressed forward the plan therefore of strengthening all the features of the government which gave it resemblance to an English constitution, of adopting the English forms & principles of administration, and of forming like them a monied interest, by means of a funding system, not calculated to pay the public debt, but to render it perpetual, and to make it an engine in the hands of the executive branch of the government which, added to the great patronage it possessed in the disposal of public offices, might enable it to assume by degrees a kingly authority. The biennial period of Congress being too short to betray to the people, spread over this great continent, this train of things during the first Congress, little change was made in the members to the second. But in the mean time two very distinct parties had formed in Congress; and before the third election, the people in general became apprised of the game which was playing for drawing over them a kind of government which they never had in contemplation. At the 3d. election therefore a decided majority of Republicans were sent to the lower house of Congress; and as information spread still farther among the people after the 4th. election the anti-republicans have become a weak minority. But the members of the Senate being changed but once in 6. years, the completion of that body will be much slower in it's assimilation to that of the people. This will account for the differences which may appear in the proceedings & spirit of the two houses. Still however it is inevitable that the Senate will at length be formed to the republican model of the people, & the two houses of the legislature, once brought to act on the true principles of the Constitution, backed by the people, will be able to defeat the plan of sliding us into monarchy, & to keep the Executive within Republican bounds, notwithstanding the immense patronage it possesses in the disposal of public offices, notwithstanding it has been able to draw into this vortex the judiciary branch of the government & by their expectancy of sharing the other offices in the Executive gift to make them auxiliary to the Executive in all it's views instead of forming a balance between that & the legislature as it was originally intended and notwithstanding the funding phalanx which a respect for public faith must protect, tho' it was engaged by false brethren. Two parties then do exist within the U.S. they embrace respectively the following descriptions of persons.

The Anti-republicans consist of

1. The old refugees & tories.

2. British merchants residing among us, & composing the main body of our merchants.

3. American merchants trading on British capital. Another great portion.

4. Speculators & Holders in the banks & public funds.

5. Officers of the federal government with some exceptions.

6. Office-hunters, willing to give up principles for places. A numerous & noisy tribe.

7. Nervous persons, whose languid fibres have more analogy with a passive than active state of things.

The Republican part of our Union comprehends

1. The entire body of landholders throughout the United States.

2. The body of labourers, not being landholders, whether in husbanding or the arts.

The latter is to the aggregate of the former party probably as 500 to one; but their wealth is not as disproportionate, tho' it is also greatly superior, and is in truth the foundation of that of their antagonists. Trifling as are the numbers of the Anti-republican party, there are circumstances which give them an appearance of strength & numbers. They all live in cities, together, & can act in a body readily & at all times; they give chief employment to the newspapers, & therefore have most of them under their command. The Agricultural interest is dispersed over a great extent of country, have little means of intercommunication with each other, and feeling their own strength & will, are conscious that a single exertion of these will at any time crush the machinations against their government. . . .

Thomas Jefferson

"FOOLISH ACTS," EARLY 1800's

The excerpt from one of Jefferson's letters, quoted below, reflects the intense passions that characterized politics in the early national period. The Federalists, Jefferson asserted, were complaining they lost the election of 1800 because the Republicans had "lied them out of power." Contrary to the Federalists' claims, Jefferson argued that their "foolish acts" had resulted in defeat. To what may we attribute the Federalists' loss of popular following: the "progress of licentiousness" which Fisher Ames feared, or the arrogance and extravagance which Jefferson maintains was theirs?

YOU will have seen by our newspapers, that with the aid of a lying renegado from republicanism, the federalists have opened all their sluices of calumny. They say we lied them out of power, and openly avow they will do the same by us. But it was not lies or argument on our part which dethroned them, but their own foolish acts, sedition laws, alien laws, taxes, extravagance & heresies. Porcupine, their friend, wrote them down. Callender, their new recruit, will do the same. Every decent man among them revolts at his filth; and there cannot be a doubt, that were a Presidential election to come on this day, they would have but three New England States, and about half a dozen votes from Maryland & North Carolina; these two States electing by districts. Were all the States to elect by a general ticket, they would have but 3 out of 16 States. And these 3 are coming up slowly. We do, indeed, consider Jersey & Delaware as rather doubtful. Elections which have lately taken place there, but their event not yet known here, will show the present point of their varying condition.

From Paul Leicester Ford, ed., *The Works of Thomas Jefferson* (New York, 1905), Vol. IX, pp. 397–398.

Robert Troup

POSSIBLE CONSEQUENCES OF FAILURE

Robert Troup (1757–1832), a New York Federalist, was most pessimistic about the possible consequences of a Republican victory at the polls in 1800. Like most Federalists, Troup took an apocalyptic view of politics and predicted a social revolution if his party lost the election. Although other Federalists feared an uprising by the lower classes, Troup envisaged a racial revolt by Negro slaves resulting from the libertarian views of the Republicans and their French supporters. Why did the Federalists believe so fervently that their defeat would prove so catastrophic? What was the link, if any, between the Jeffersonian Republicans and revolutionary France?

MY good friend, I cannot describe to you how broken and scattered your federal friends are! At present we have no rallying point; and no mortal can divine where or when we shall again collect our strength! . . . Shadows, clouds, and darkness rest on our future prospects. My spirits, in spite of all my philosophy, cannot maintain the accustomed level. For the present they have sunk me into an apathy for public concern, and forced me into the bosom of my own family—where after all is centered the only happiness we can expect to enjoy on earth.

In Virginia they are beginning to feel the happy effects of liberty and equality. A serious and tremendous insurrection was on the point of breaking out there a few days ago. It was discovered as it was about being executed. The reports from that quarter say that it was planned by Frenchmen, and that all the whites, save the French, were to have been sacrificed. The whole state has been in consternation—their courts are sitting—trials are taking place and the gallows are in full operation. . . . We are also told that there actually has been a rising of negroes in South Carolina. . . .

Genl. Armstrong is said to be Jefferson's religious champion. . . . Hamilton thinks worse of the state of our affairs than I do. I cannot bring myself to believe that the same consequences will result which he apprehends. . . .

From Charles R. King, ed., *The Life and Correspondence of Rufus King* . . . (New York, 1896), Vol. III, pp. 315–316.

II. CONTROVERSY AMONG HISTORIANS

Richard B. Morris

HAMILTON AS REALIST

Richard B. Morris, a leading scholar of the Revolution and Confederation periods, pictures Alexander Hamilton as a political realist who worked out a brilliant plan to unify support for the newly-founded central government. Hamilton, according to Morris, was one of America's first great nationalists: a statesman who recognized that the good of the country demanded that the interests of the upper class be welded to the central government if the nation was to survive and prosper. But if Hamilton was such a political realist, would he have taken a gamble which might alienate the vast majority of the electorate—the small farmers—in order to secure the support of a minority—the privileged upper class?

AS he was about to assume the office of the Presidency George Washington remarked to a friend: "My movements to the chair of government will be accompanied by feelings not unlike those of a culprit who is going to the place of his execution." Washington's observation was indeed prophetic. Since the days of the Founding Fathers America's great public figures have been the recipients of much uncritical adulation and the targets of fierce vilification. They have been placed on a pedestal or kicked in the gutter. They have become transfigured into mythological heroes with saint-like attributes or into rascals whose motives have been impugned, whose personal lives have been invaded, and whose achievements belittled and distorted.

The career of Alexander Hamilton is an outstanding illustration of this ironic phenomenon of American politics. Endowed with exceptional precocity, consuming energy, and high ambition, Hamilton stood in the center of events from the earliest days of the Revolution until the late years of President Adams' administration. In the course of his pub-

lic career he accumulated a wide variety of enemies. John Adams called him "the bastard brat of a Scots peddler." Jefferson charged him with being "not only a monarchist, but for a monarchy bottomed on corruption." The hired scribbler, Callender, defamed him as a Caligula, and Senator Maclay called him a crook. Since his own day he has been assailed as an enemy of democracy, a friend of reaction, an ally of the special interests, a High Tory who sought to erect a leviathan state, and an archplotter against the life of the republic.

That such charges were groundless was the sober judgment of many of Hamilton's contemporaries. Washington, perhaps Hamilton's greatest admirer and certainly his chief disciple, paid tribute to his enterprise, his quick perception, and "his judgment intuitively great." Granted that Hamilton was ambitious, Washington considered that his ambition was "of that laudable kind, which prompts a man to excel in whatever he takes in hand." The worldly Talleyrand, who knew him well, bracketed Hamilton with Napoleon and Fox. These three he considered the outstand-

From Richard B. Morris, *Alexander Hamilton and the Founding of the Nation* (New York: Dial Press, 1957), pp. VII–XIII. Reprinted by permission of the author.

ing figures of that epoch. One political opponent conceded that Hamilton, "more than any other man, did the thinking of the time."

That Hamilton should have become a symbol of party, class, and faction is one of the ironies of American history. No man of his generation accomplished more to break down local barriers and sectional prejudices which had hampered the formation of a strong union. Save Washington, no man was more opposed to the spirit of party and faction. Yet, the Hamiltonian program fomented both the party spirit and partisanship. Hamilton did not foresee that the two-party system would prove a stabilizing force in American government. To him party was synonymous with disorder and instability.

Hamilton was one of our first great nationalists. "Think continentally," he counseled the young nation. He believed in the destiny of America and wished to confer upon the national government powers appropriate to its needs and opportunities. In *The Federalist* he shows how such national unity could be achieved without sacrificing states' rights and without jeopardizing individual liberties. His interpretation of the Constitution was both audacious and masterly. His enunciation of the doctrine of implied powers gave the nationalist Supreme Court the arguments for that broad construction which they put upon the Constitution. His interpretation of the taxing power opened up to the federal government sources of revenue essential to its needs prior to the adoption of the income tax amendment. A stanch advocate of separation of powers and checks and balances, Hamilton asserted the independence of the judiciary, and, of all the Founding Fathers, was most forceful in arguing for the right of the Supreme Court to declare laws of Congress unconstitutional. He believed that the courts were the safeguard of minority rights, and was confident that curbs upon judicial usurpation existed in the Constitution.

Hamilton was an administrative genius, perhaps the greatest America has yet produced. He believed in a strong executive, guarded the Presidency from encroachments upon its power by the legislative branch of the government, and assumed an influence in Washington's cabinet which is unmatched in the annals of the American cabinet system. Concerning himself with every phase of public policy, he was more than merely Secretary of the Treasury. He was in fact Washington's prime minister.

Hamilton's inventive mind grasped an extraordinary range of governmental problems—constitutional, economic, diplomatic, and military. His fiscal program was bold, original, and constructive, and firmly established American credit at home and abroad. To do so, he created a national debt and made effective use of the government's taxing power. With pardonable rhetoric Daniel Webster spoke of Hamilton's achievements: "He smote the rock of national resources and abundant streams of revenue gushed forth; he touched the dead corpse of public credit and it sprang upon its feet." The program injected confidence and buoyancy into the business community, but was received with less enthusiasm in other quarters. Farmers, small shopkeepers, and craftsmen saw little immediate advantage to them in the funding operations and rallied to Jefferson's opposition standard.

Hamilton was the friend of business enterprise, but he believed that business should be regulated in the interest of the general welfare, that competition should be fostered and monopoly discouraged. He did not subscribe to the view that business was not the business of government. Believing as he did in a government possessed with energy and initiative, he could scarcely be expected to allow the government to stand inert while the economy stagnated or was stifled by foreign competition. Hamilton advocated a nationally directed and controlled economy in the interest of private enterprise. He believed that the economy should be invigorated and protected by bounties and tariffs, by canals, roads, and other public improvements built by the federal government, and "by opening an asylum" to the poor and oppressed of other lands. He believed in maintaining a sound credit, in keeping the national debt within bounds, but he could scarcely be called a hard money man, and would today be considered an advocate of a managed currency. He recognized that private enterprise was subject to abuse. He castigated bank abuses as "pernicious," and insisted that "public utility" was "more truly the object of public banks than private profit."

Hamilton's remarkable grasp of national interest was evident in the direction he gave to the foreign policy of the Washington administration. He was a realist. He saw nothing "absurd" or "impracticable" in a league or alliance of nations, but cautioned Americans against becoming "the instruments of European greatness." He believed that a power friendly today could become an enemy tomorrow, "that peace or war will not always be left to our option." At the time of Jay's Treaty he opposed war with Great Britain because in his judgment a cessation of trade would "cut up credit by the roots," and above all because America needed time. It was too young and weak to involve itself in European wars. These ideas were given expression in Washington's Farewell Address, which in final form drew substantially upon Hamilton's "original draft." Hamilton's guiding principles were prudence, realism, discretion in speech, moderation in action, concern for the national interest. "Real firmness is good for every thing," he once counseled. "Strut is good for nothing."

Hamilton was an extraordinary advocate. As a speaker he was less effective with crowds than with assemblies and in the courtroom. He was an orator in the tradition for Pitt, Fox, and Burke. It was the kind of oratory that changed votes and persuaded judges. But it was as an essayist rather than an orator that Hamilton was most persuasive. *The Federalist* has justly become the classic of constitutional analysis and reasoning. Hamilton's *Phocion, Camillus,* and *Pacificus* letters are other powerful examples of a form of polemical writing that has unfortunately vanished from the literary scene. Flattering his readers by

his appeal to logic and reason, Hamilton moved them to action by powerful emotional arguments. It need hardly be added that Hamilton wrote his own speeches and state papers. He did not need other men to fabricate ideas for him or ghost writers to dress them in literary garb.

It has been the fashion to pin the label of conservatism upon Hamilton, and in many respects he was profoundly conservative. But the program he, along with Madison, advocated in the Confederation period—the establishment of a strong national government, the creation of a new kind of republican federalism —was profoundly radical. It constituted a sharp break with the political ways of the past to which his opponents, the die-hard states'-rights particularists, wished to adhere.

Hamilton's brand of conservatism meant holding on to the tried and proven values of the past, but not standing still. He was not afraid of the new and the experimental. "There are epochs in human affairs when *novelty* even is useful," when "a change is necessary, if it be but for the sake of change," he wrote in advocating his program of Continental reforms as early as 1780. Hamilton believed in change and progress, but he hoped change would come by evolution rather than by volcanic eruption. There was, then, nothing paradoxical about the fact that Hamilton was an ardent defender of the American Revolution and an equally ardent foe of the French Revolution. The former, in Hamilton's eyes, was a political revolution actuated by principles of law, justice, and moderation, whereas the French Revolution, as he saw it, became a class struggle, employing violence and terror, and seeking imperialist ends through military aggrandisement.

Hamilton's enlightened conservatism, his devotion to "the mild reign of rational liberty," is perhaps best exemplified by his desire to conserve civil liberties, by his attachment to due process, to trial by jury, to the freedom of the press, and to the rights of minorities. He opposed loyalty oaths, indiscriminate confiscation of property, and religious tests

for voting. "Let us not establish a tyranny," he warned at the time the Sedition Act was being considered by Congress.

In the last analysis it is the enduring
quality of Hamilton's program which
provides the true measure of his greatness as a statesman. Hamilton's suc-
cessors in office found that his fiscal
policies could not be rudely dethroned.
"We can pay off his debts in fifteen
years, but we can never get rid of his
financial system," Jefferson grimly confessed on ascending to the Presidency.
To justify the most significant accom-
plishment of his administration—the
purchase of Louisiana—Jefferson had
to adopt Hamilton's broad construction
of the Constitution. Since that day the
difference between the broad and the
strict constructionists, between the Hamiltonians and the Jeffersonians, has been
in large measure a difference between
the party in power with responsibility
and the party out of power and in opposition. Jefferson might have explained
this philosophically by reminding us
that "every difference of opinion is not
a difference of principle."

Jefferson wanted "a wise and frugal
government." Hamilton wanted a government that could act. Wars, unem-
ployment, and the complexities and
tensions of modern civilization have
steadily foisted upon government new
and awesome responsibilities. Woodrow
Wilson once put the issue quite suc-
cintly:

We used to think in the old-fashioned days
when life was very simple that all government had to do was to put on a policeman's
uniform, and say, "Now don't anybody hurt
anybody else." We used to say that the ideal
of government was for every man to be left
alone and not interfered with, except when
he interfered with somebody else; and that
the best government was the government
that did as little governing as possible. That
was the idea that obtained in Jefferson's
time. But we are coming now to realize that
life is so complicated that we are not dealing with the old conditions, and that the law
has to step in and create new conditions
under which we may live, the conditions
which will make it tolerable for us to live.

The ends of government to which Wilson was pointing have in the course of
time ranged beyond the vision of the
Founding Fathers, but the means of
achieving them are orthodox Hamiltonian means. Today neither of the two
great parties would venture to challenge
the effective exercise of political power
for the general welfare. Were Alexander
Hamilton alive in the mid-twentieth
century he would find that both parties
accept as axiomatic the Hamiltonian
proposition that the central government
must have effective powers.

In his Army Pay Book Hamilton, as a
young Revolutionary officer, made various notes and jotted down a variety of
quotations. One of them is surprisingly
self-revealing. It is from an oration of
Demosthenes, and, as entered by Hamilton, reads: "As a general marches at
the head of his troops, so ought wise
politicians, if I dare use the expression,
to march at the head of affairs; insomuch that they ought not to wait the
event, to know what measures to take;
but the measures which they have taken
ought to produce the event."

Truly it may be said that Hamilton
constantly seized the initiative and kept
ahead of events. Talleyrand said of
Hamilton, "he has anticipated Europe."
It may with as much accuracy be asserted that he anticipated America. The
prophetic nature of much of Hamilton's
thinking seems positively uncanny. It
was Richard Rush, a Secretary of the
Treasury from the opposition party, who
paid tribute to Hamilton's direction of
operations of the Treasury "with a fore-
cast so luminous as still to throw a guiding light over the path of his succes-
sors." Hamilton envisioned America as
a great industrial giant, whose manufacturing output would raise the general
standard of living and stimulate both
commerce and agriculture. Hamilton
believed that the nation must be put
into a strong posture of defense, that we
could not rely upon the long-range peaceful intentions of foreign powers or count
upon permanent alliances. He even
warned of wars starting by surprise attacks without the formality of a declara-

tion. Hamilton's alertness to the dangers of nullification, interposition, and secession take on sombre overtones in the light of later history. An advocate of the supremacy of the union, his views were to be upheld by Jackson and vindicated by Lincoln. Hamilton anticipated the later assumption by the Supreme Court of powers for the federal government on the basis of three clauses in the Constitution—the necessary and proper clause, the general welfare clause, and the commerce clause. These three clauses, as Hamilton interpreted them, have provided the constitutional foundation for much of the activity of our modern federal government in the fields of taxation, finance, business regulation, and social welfare, activities undreamed of when the nation was in its infancy. To Hamilton the enormous expansion of the power of the Presidency by the mid-twentieth century would have been less a surprise than a vindication of his notions of the need for administrative power, energy, and efficiency.

Hamilton's failures as a statesman are attributable more to personality and tactics than to basic principles. Hamilton carried courage in politics to the point of self-immolation. If there was any attacking to be done, he did not assign the task to someone else, but took it on himself. As Jefferson put it, he was truly the "Colossus of the Federalists," and the standing No. 1 target for the shafts of the opposition. Opinionated and self-assured, he lacked that understanding of the art of compromise, the mastery of which is so essential to the aspiring politician. Thus, he was inflexible when a little yielding would have made all the difference. The best example of this was his break with Madison over the question of discriminating between original and subsequent holders of public securities. Though probably impractical in operation, some sort of discrimination would have seemed fair and equitable and would certainly have been good politics. Hamilton lacked terminal facilities. He was candid, but he was also indiscreet. He wrote brilliantly, but he wrote too much and too often. His astonishing attack on President John Adams left Hamilton a party leader without a following.

With some justice it has been said that Hamilton loved his country more than he did his countrymen. He would not bow to what he called "the majesty of the multitude." Direct democracy, he felt, was unsuitable to a large nation like America. It would, he feared, prove tumultuous and fickle. But he was reconciled to the system of representative democracy set up in the Constitution. Although an admirer of the British constitution, he realized that only a republic was suited to the American temper. While Hamilton was often portrayed by his opponents as an enemy of the people, the fact is that he was less afraid of the people than he was of state political machines and state legislatures. In Hamilton's thinking the loyalty of the people to the national government was an essential weapon to counteract the separatist and divisive tactics of the antifederalists. It must be confessed that there were times when Hamilton had his doubts about the way democracy was working out, and that he was understandably less enthusiastic about democracy when his party was voted out of office than when it was in power. But he believed in the power of reason founded upon full disclosure of the facts, and he had faith in the force of an enlightened public opinion. "I desire above all things," he wrote, "to see the equality of political rights, exclusive of hereditary distinction, firmly established by a postive demonstration of its being consistent with the order and happiness of society."

Cecelia M. Kenyon

HAMILTON: ROUSSEAU OF THE RIGHT

Cecelia M. Kenyon, contrary to Richard B. Morris, sees Hamilton as the supreme idealist—the epitome of 18th-century Enlightenment thought. Although she agrees with Morris that Hamilton sought to strengthen the central government by gaining the support of elite elements in American society, Kenyon attributes Hamilton's motivation to his deep-seated philosophical assumptions. Hamilton, she claims, believed in Rousseau's concept of the general will or the public good, and that such public good both in moral and political terms should come before the private interests of the individual. Kenyon argues further that Hamilton's brand of idealism was alien to the prevailing will of the majority of Americans. For these reasons his views were not accepted by his countrymen. Was Hamilton's inability to reconcile his views with the political realities of the period a sign of strong-willed idealism, or simply arrogance?

THE thesis of this paper is suggested in the title. It is that Hamilton's political thought was characterized by a heavy emphasis on a concept central to Rousseau's theory, the general will or the public good; that for Hamilton, as for Rousseau, this public good was morally and politically prior to private, individual ends, with which it was occasionally if not frequently in conflict; that the content of this public good as Hamilton visualized it was alien to the prevailing will of the majority of Americans in the early years of the Republic; that Hamilton was never able to reconcile his political ideal with his announced view of political reality; and that, as a result, his political theory is confused, contradictory, and basically unrealistic.

It is no light matter to charge Alexander Hamilton with a lack of realism. His writings are filled with references to what has been called the "dark side of humanity"; none of his contemporaries excelled him in constant emphasis on self-interest as man's dominant political motive, or in warnings against the evil passions of man's nature. Every undergraduate knows that Hamilton had a "pessimistic" conception of human nature. Every undergraduate knows, too, that the new government established under the Constitution desperately needed its finances put in order, and that Hamilton accomplished this. How, then, can such a man be called unrealistic? My argument is that Hamilton was not able to accept with equanimity the political facts of life as he saw them, or to relate them successfully to the political ideals he pursued. There remained within his thought an unresolved tension between what he believed man was, and what he believed man ought to be. Such a tension is not of course unusual, but the distance between the *is* and the *ought* in Hamilton's ideas was extreme.

This tension can best be examined by comparing the Hamilton of the Federal Convention with the Hamilton of the Federalist party. They are the same man, but not quite the same thinker.

In his speech of June 18, 1787, Hamilton presented his plan of a political system proper for America. He wanted to do two things: to transfer the attachment of the people from the governments of their separate states to that of the Union; and to construct that government in such a way that it would not

From Cecelia M. Kenyon, "Alexander Hamilton: Rousseau of the Right." Reprinted with permission from the *Political Science Quarterly* (June, 1958), Vol. LXXIII, No. 2. pp. 161–179.

be wrecked by the turbulence of democracy and the imprudence of the people.

In the first part of the speech Hamilton analyzed those "great and essential principles necessary for the support of government," and found that all of them then operated in favor of the states rather than of the Union. These principles of political obedience were several —interest, love of power, habit, force, influence. In order to make them support the nation rather than the separate states, Hamilton advocated an almost complete transfer of sovereignty from the latter governments to the former. This proposal is significant because of its apparent assumption that those very passions by which the people were so strongly attached to their state governments might remain sufficiently quiescent to permit the reduction of the states to the position of administrative provinces. It was the most drastic proposal of Hamilton's career and suggests his affinity with the classical tradition of the Legislator as well as his propensity—usually restrained—for Draconian measures.

In the second part of the speech Hamilton defended that part of his plan which provided for a senate and an executive elected for life. These were to serve as checks on the people's will, which would be represented in a popularly elected lower house with limited tenure. The reports of Madison and Yates differ somewhat, and for that reason I shall quote both versions of the crucial passage, beginning with that of Madison.

In every community where industry is encouraged, there will be a division of it into the few and the many. Hence, separate interests will arise. There will be debtors and creditors, etc. Give all power to the many, they will oppress the few. Give all power to the few, they will oppress the many. Both, therefore, ought to have the power, that each may defend itself against the other. To the want of this check we owe our paper-money instalment laws, etc. To the proper adjustment of it the British owe the excellence of their constitution. Their House of Lords is a most noble institution. Having

nothing to hope for by a change, and a sufficient interest, by means of their property, in being faithful to the national interest, they form a permanent barrier against every pernicious innovation whether attempted on the part of the Crown or of the Commons. No temporary Senate will have firmness enough to answer the purpose.

All communities divide themselves into the few and the many. The first are the rich and well-born, the other the mass of the people. The voice of the people has been said to be the voice of God; and however generally this maxim has been quoted and believed, it is not true in fact. The people are turbulent and changing; they seldom judge or determine right. Give, therefore, to the first class a distinct, permanent share in the government. They will check the unsteadiness of the second, and, as they cannot receive any advantage by a change, they therefore will ever maintain good government. Can a democratic Assembly, who annually revolve in the mass of the people, be supposed steadily to pursue the public good? Nothing but a permanent body can check the imprudence of democracy. Their turbulence and uncontrolling disposition requires checks.

I believe these statements constitute the cornerstone of Hamilton's theory. They were made in the course of debates not intended for publication, and in defense of a system which Hamilton should have known had little chance of being adopted. Here Hamilton was his own advocate, not, as in *The Federalist*, advocate of a system which he believed to be less than second best. These statements, therefore, require careful explication.

There is, to begin with, the familiar division of men into the few and the many, or the rich and the well-born, and the mass of the people. There is the further assumption that the interests of these two classes will be different, that they will be in conflict with each other at least part of the time, that the political behavior of each class will be motivated by its interests, and that each class will oppress the other if it gets the chance and has the power to do so. Hamilton does not want this last to happen: "Both, therefore, ought to have the power, that each may defend itself against the other." It was not, then, a class government that Hamilton sought, at least not in the sense of one that had as its end the direct and deliberate promotion of class interests.

Thus far, there is no real difficulty in interpreting Hamilton. But the remainder of the passage, whether as reported by Madison or Yates, is less clear because it is, or appears to be, elliptical. In the second part of the passage, Hamilton suggests that the few will be more reliable in the cause of good government than the many. They, then, should have a share in the governing process, not only to protect their class interests, but in order to secure the national interest. Why will the few be the better guardians of this interest than the many? There seem to be two reasons, though neither is fully expounded.

In both the Madison and Yates versions, Hamilton expresses hostility to change and implies, if he does not explicitly state, that change is inimical to the "national interest" (Madison) or "good government" (Yates). This attitude is accompanied by the assertion that the upper class will be opposed to change. Therefore, the upper class will be the safer guardian of the public interest, not because its members are fundamentally more virtuous than "the people," but because on this particular issue—of change—their separate, class interest coincides with the public interest. It is also suggested (in the Madison but not in the Yates version) that the property of the Lords keeps that body faithful to the national interest in Britain.

This is a curious and revealing passage. Consider first the attitude toward change. It seems inconsistent with most of Hamilton's own career, for who among his contemporaries was more constantly in the vanguard of reform than he? He was an ardent Revolutionist; he was wholeheartedly in support of the movement for a new Constitution; his proposals as Secretary of the Treasury envisioned a deliberate effort to effect profound changes in the nature of American society; and the very speech in which he expressed this hostility to change was the speech in which he was

recommending changes in the existing system far too drastic for his colleagues to accept. In comparison, the fluctuating policies followed by some of the states between 1776 and 1787, and which were so deplored by Hamilton and the other delegates, were the merest piddling. Hamilton was not alone in his quest for stability, but the attitude expressed in this speech, coupled with his own ardent support of sweeping changes, does call for a bit of explaining.

Again, I think, it reveals Hamilton as the modern prototype of the Legislator: take whatever measures are necessary to establish good Laws, and then guard against the undermining forces of future change. It is an attitude which cannot be reconciled with the theory of conservatism expounded by Burke three years later, for not only does it call for radical reconstruction, but it is hostile to the gradual, piecemeal process of adaptation which Burke accepted as characteristic of the natural life of society.

Consider next the assumption implicit in the relationship Hamilton posited between the national interest, the interest of the upper classes, good government, and an inclination or disinclination toward change. He assumes, first, that change is not compatible with good government. He assumes, second, that the upper classes will not be inclined toward change. These two assumptions are explicit. There is a third assumption which is implicit: good government is that which favors or protects the interests of these classes, but not the interests of the many—for it is they who are most likely to advocate change. It is therefore difficult to escape the conclusion that no matter how pure and patriotic Hamilton was in intent, he nevertheless tended to associate good government and the national interest with the interest of the rich, the well-born, and the few.

The exact nature of this relationship is difficult to pin down. The national interest is apparently regarded as both different from and separate from that of the many, and different from though not always separate from that of the few. It is, in short, distinct. It is the Hamiltonian counterpart of the Rousseauan general will, that will of the community toward its corporate good, something quite distinct from the will of all, which is the sum of individual and group private, self-interested wills. For Hamilton, this national interest was the primary end of government.

What we are concerned with here, then, is the fundamental question in any political theory: the end of government. It is a question which was not much discussed during the debate over ratification, and its answer was assumed and accepted rather than reached by any genuinely searching analysis even during the Revolutionary debate. This answer was more or less ready-made, and packaged in the doctrine of natural law and natural rights. Now this doctrine is ambivalent in its implications with respect to individuals and social unity. If the emphasis is on natural *law*, as it was during the medieval period, the doctrine tends in the direction of harmony and consensus. But if the emphasis is on *rights*, and especially if happiness is included among the rights, then the doctrine tends toward individualism. It cannot do otherwise, and it was no mere whim which led Rousseau to reject natural rights doctrine as the basis for his state.

Some political thinkers in America in the eighteenth century realized the ethical implications of their accepted doctrine quite fully, and others did not. Jefferson was among those who did. His poetic passages on the virtues of agrarianism really boil down to a belief that this way of life was the one in which men could most easily fulfill their self-interest without being driven to do so by means which corrupted their integrity or injured their fellows. If Jefferson had an "optimistic" view of human nature, it was because his expectations and hopes were limited not only by a recognition of egoism but by an acceptance of it as ethically legitimate.

Tom Paine, though fully committed to the doctrine of natural rights as a justification for freedom, was not aware of and was not committed to its egoistic ethical implications. Thus his apologia for unicameralism:

My idea of a single legislature was always founded on a hope, that whatever personal parties might be in the state, they would all unite and agree in the general principles of good government—that these party differences would be dropped at the threshold of the state house, and that the public good, or the good of the whole, would be the governing principle of the legislature within it.

Party dispute, taken on this ground, would only be, who should have the honor of making the laws; not what the laws should be.

Implicit in this lost hope is the Rousseauan concept of the ideal citizen, he who distinguishes between his private interest and the public good, suppresses the former, and votes wholeheartedly for the latter.

It is my belief that this was also Hamilton's ideal, that he never abandoned it as the standard for judging political behavior, even though he fully realized that it was not in accord with the facts of human nature. This standard, essentially a non-liberal standard, was the springboard of his bitter attacks on the reason and virtue of the people. Thus I would argue that the real difference between Hamilton's and Jefferson's conceptions of human nature and their respective estimates of the people's capacity for self-government lay not in what either believed man actually to be, but in what each thought man ought to be and do. As far as politics was concerned, Jefferson thought man should pursue his happiness; Hamilton thought he should seek the national interest. One called for egoistic behavior, the other for altruistic. It was Hamilton who was the greater idealist, Jefferson the greater realist.

Yet Hamilton strove mightily for realism. His method was ambitious, arrogant, and in the great tradition of Plato, Machiavelli and Rousseau. It was the method of the Legislator. The following passages indicate the spirit of Hamilton's belief that man's nature could and should be molded for his own good as well as for that of the state.

Take mankind in general, they are vicious, their passions may be operated upon. . . . Take mankind as they are, and what are they governed by? Their passions. There may be in every government a few choice spirits, who may act from more worthy motives. One great error is that we suppose mankind more honest than they are. Our prevailing passions are ambition and interest; and *it will ever be the duty of a wise government to avail itself of the passions, in order to make them subservient to the public good; for these ever induce us to action.*

The true politician . . . takes human nature (and human society its aggregate) as he finds it, a compound of good and ill qualities, of good and ill tendencies. . . .

With this view of human nature he will not attempt to warp or disturb from its natural direction, he will not attempt to promote its happiness by means to which it is not suited . . . but he will seek to promote his action according to the bias of his nature, to lead him to the development of his energies according to the scope of his passions, and erecting the social organization on this basis he will favor all those institutions and plans which tend to make men happy according to their natural bent, which multiply the sources of individual enjoyment and increase of national resources and strength.

This is the spirit of the Legislator, though, to be sure, infinitely less ruthless than that of Plato or Rousseau. It implies wisdom on the one hand, malleability on the other, and an essentially manipulative relationship between the two. In modern times this sort of thing goes by the name of social engineering. Before and during the eighteenth century, it was usually associated with some form of benevolent despotism. Hamilton's problem, like Rousseau's, was to adapt it to republican government. The difficulty for each was the same: the people had the power but not the wisdom, while the leaders had the wisdom but not the power. How, then, could the people be made to follow wisdom? Rousseau's answer was simple: let the Legislator claim for his plans the authority of the gods.

Hamilton's answer was not so simple. *The Federalist Papers* were an appeal to reason, to self-interest, and to patriotism. Most of his other publicist ventures were similar. In spite of all his diatribes about the weakness of man's reason and the dominance of man's passions, Hamilton never abandoned hope that the better side of man's nature might be reached and might respond. Even the misguided *Caesar Letters*, if indeed they were his, represented an appeal to the people's reason. This was the idealist in Hamilton, relatively pure and certainly indestructible.

His financial program both reveals and represents the other major facet in his answer to the problem of the Legislator. It reflects Hamilton the blundering realist. It is sometimes said that, having failed to secure a permanent share in the structure of government for the upper classes, Hamilton sought to secure their attachment to the new government through his financial program. I believe this is correct. It was a long-term policy and it is succinctly stated in a sentence chosen by Professor Morris to head one of the selections in his excellent anthology. "The only plan that can preserve the currency is one that will make it the *immediate* interest of the moneyed men to cooperate with government in its support." The emphasis on the word *immediate* was Hamilton's. Nearly a decade passed after this was written before he became Secretary of the Treasury, and during that period his fiscal theories were elaborated and matured. But the basic principle remained the same: the private interest of the moneyed class must be made the ally of the national interest. Selfish interest must be made to support the public good. And how? By having the moneyed class's bread buttered by the government. There would, then, be no conflict between its interest and the general welfare. So far, so good. By catering to its self-interest, one class is led to do what is right. This is a fine exercise in political realism.

But what of the other class, the "many" of the June 18th speech in the Convention? In that speech Hamilton implied, though he did not explicitly state, that the interests of the two classes, the few and the many, would be in conflict with each other. Logically, then, any policy which served the interests of the few would injure or at least jeopardize the interests of the many. It is true that Hamilton believed that his fiscal policies would serve the national interest, and it is also true that he believed they would ultimately serve the self-interest of the many. But he *did* emphasize the necessity of attaching the *immediate* interest of the moneyed class to the government, and he had stated, in *The Federalist,* that men in general were much more likely to act in accordance with what they believed to be their immediate interests than their long-run interests. Logically, therefore, he ought to have expected widespread opposition to the policies he advocated as Secretary of the Treasury, and equally logically he ought to have accepted such opposition with equanimity.

That he did not is well known. His letters and papers of the 1790's are filled with blasts against Jefferson, blasts against the people, blasts against factionalism, and laments about the lack of patriotism in everyone except himself and a few kindred Federalists. Hamilton was genuinely shocked, and he should really not have been. For consider what he had done. In his Convention speech he had posited the existence of two classes, with probably conflicting interests. In the Convention and elsewhere—innumerable times—he had argued that men are dominated by self-interest. He had occasionally, though not consistently, suggested that the upper classes were more likely to be patriotic than the mass of the people. Nevertheless, he had sought the support of this group, not by appealing to their patriotism, altruism, or even long-run interest, but by appealing deliberately to their *immediate* self-interest. It was to them that he held out the carrot. And it was the other class, the many, the mass of the people, upon whom he now called for patriotism, and/or appreciation of long-run self-interest. It was from this class that he now expected and demanded the greater exercise of both reason and virtue. In so doing, he was not logical, he was not realistic,

and he led his party straight down the road to extinction.

There were times during the late 1790's and early 1800's when he half-realized what he had done and cast about for practical solutions. In 1799 he advocated road-building as a method of courting the people's good will. It was a measure "universally popular." He also advocated the institution of a society with funds for the encouragement of agriculture and the arts. Such a program, he wrote, would "speak powerfully to the feelings and interests of those classes of men to whom the benefits derived from the government have been heretofore the least manifest."

Before commenting on this proposal, I should like to place beside it a passage from another attempt by Hamilton to explain his party's failure to win popular support.

Nothing is more fallacious than to expect to produce any valuable or permanent result in political projects by relying merely on the reason of men. Men are rather reasoning than reasonable animals, for the most part governed by the impulse of passion. This is a truth well understood by our adversaries, who have practised upon it with no small benefit to their cause; for at the very moment they are eulogizing the reason of men, and professing to appeal only to that faculty, they are courting the strongest and most active passion of the human heart, vanity! It is no less true, that the Federalists seem not to have attended to the fact sufficiently; and that they erred in relying so much on the rectitude and utility of their measures as to have neglected the cultivation of popular favor, by fair and justifiable expedients.

These comments reveal the very deep conflict in Hamilton's thought. In the later one (1802), Hamilton saw his party's error in having relied "so much on the rectitude and utility of their measures, as to have neglected the cultivation of popular favor, by fair and justifiable expedients." In the earlier letter, Hamilton admitted that the benefits of the new government had thus far not been "manifest" to certain classes —in the context, the many. In both letters, the two Hamiltons show through:

the idealist, sure of the rightness of his policies and regretful that the people were neither rational nor virtuous enough to accept them on their merits; the realist, ever ready to seek support by the enlistment of man's worse (but never worst) nature. He had deliberately done the latter to win the moneyed class over to his side in the early 1790's. Now, at the end of the decade, he proposed to do the same thing for the majority. But it was a classic case of too little, too late. He had, in effect, made a partnership between the national interest and a special class interest. I am not sure whether he intended this partnership to be permanent and exclusive. He did intend it to be universally benevolent; its fruits were meant to trickle down and be enjoyed by everyone. Yet there remains that implicit assumption of the June 18th speech: a desire for change is more likely to exist among the many than the few, because good government will leave the interests of the many unsatisfied. There is an ambivalence in Hamilton's theory which I find it impossible to resolve.

My primary interest is not to decide whether he was or was not a class theorist, however. His political ideas are significant and rewarding because they reflect and illumine a difficult stage in the evolution of liberal democratic thought.

As I have suggested earlier, Hamilton's basic difference from Jefferson, and I think from most Americans of the era, was his rejection of the ethical egoism implicit in natural rights doctrine. This difference ought not to be exaggerated. No American of the age was an advocate of unrestrained self-interest, and the concept of a general interest which may be separate from and in conflict with private interests was generally present. It was at the root of the Revolutionary generation's distrust of faction. Nor, on the other hand, did Hamilton advocate or desire an absolute subjection of the individual to the state. It was rather that Hamilton, like Paine, was more extreme in his condemnation of egoism and in act represented an older view of the proper end of government.

This older view was pre-individualistic, pre-modern. It was the medieval view that government existed for the good of society, and its end therefore was the common good. One of the things that distinguishes modern theory from medieval is the greater difficulty modern theorists face in defining this concept, the common good. There are a number of reasons for this; among them are the greater unity of medieval society by virtue of Christianity, and the relative rôles of legislative and customary law in the governing process. The point is that the existence of a common good was assumed in the earlier period, and its content was easier to define. But introduce into the political system the concept of ethical individualism combined with the practice of legislative determination of policy, and the difficulty of defining the common good is obvious—by hindsight. It was not obvious in the sixteenth century, or the seventeenth. It became increasingly obvious to Americans in the first three quarters of the eighteenth century because they were virtually self-governing communities and met the problem in the everyday conduct of their affairs. Madison's Tenth *Federalist* was the culmination of a long and painful process of thought on this subject. Madison, and I think he was here accurately re-reflecting the dominant opinion of his contemporaries, seems to hover ambivalently between two conceptions: (1) that of an ever elusive public good somehow distinct from the clashing of selfish and private interests; (2) that of the public good as a reconciliation or compromise of these same interests.

Hamilton clung more closely to the former view. One of the reasons may have been his late arrival as a practitioner of republicanism. In this respect he was very like Tom Paine, and I think a comparison of their lives from the time of their arrival in this country will show their fundamental kinship, though one was politically of the Right, the other of the Left. Each devoted himself without reserve to the service of his country. For each of them this entailed a sacrifice of the private interests common to most men—property, or at least greater property for both, and for Hamilton, the welfare of his family. For him, the sacrifice in the end was extreme. Among the documents he wrote before the duel there is one which concludes with a sentence profoundly symbolic of his entire life. After recounting his abhorrence on the practice on religious and ethical grounds, his unwillingness to give grief to his wife and children, his feeling of responsibility to his creditors, his intention of reserving fire on the first and perhaps even the second shot, Hamilton concluded: "The ability to be in future useful, whether in resisting mischief or in effecting good, in those crises of our public affairs which seem likely to happen, would probably be inseparable from a conformity with public prejudice in this particular." He was indeed a patriot.

At every step of his career (except possibly the row with Washington), Hamilton—and Paine—put country first, self second. In a sense this was not sacrifice but fulfillment of their deepest desires. But in so far as it was fulfillment, it marked them off from other men. Each was in essence a political being, intensely so; each realized his nature, his self-interest, in devoting himself to the public good. The personality of each reinforced his conception of this public good as something better than and different from a mere reconciliation of individual and group interests. Neither ever ceased to regard his standard of political behavior as the standard proper for every man. For Paine, this meant an ever recurring optimism punctuated with bitter disillusion. For Hamilton, it meant a steady and self-nourishing pessimism. Both were idealists, and both shared the same ideal: a Rousseauistic community in which men were citizens first and individuals second. Hamilton knew his ideal was incapable of realization, and he sought a substitute which might still achieve the same goal—a government that governed in

the national interest. The substitute was an alliance of upper-class interests with the national interests.

Jefferson and Madison opposed him partly because of the nature of the alliance, partly because the content of his conception of the public good was too nationalistic for their tastes. I do not think either he or they ever fully realized the more theoretical, and I think more fundamental, difference between them. The difference was subtle but profound. Jefferson and Madison were committed to the ethical individualism implicit in natural rights theory: the end of the government as the protection of life, liberty, and the pursuit of happiness. This doctrine recognizes the political legitimacy of egoism. Hamilton was only partly committed to the doctrine. The basic difference between him and most of his contemporaries was that his conception of the public good was the older, corporate one, and theirs was the newer one in which the corporate element, though still present, had given ground to individualism.

The tension between these two concepts, a corporate and an individualistic public good, can be observed throughout the Revolutionary period. It underlay the colonial opposition to the British theory of virtual representation; it was central to the debates in the Federal Convention, and it was a major element in the ratification controversy. During the latter, James Winthrop seemed to be speaking directly to Hamilton when he wrote, "It is vain to tell us that we ought to overlook local interests. It is only by protecting local concerns that the interest of the whole is preserved." This was the spirit of the future of American politics: local interests, sectional interests, class interests, group interests, individual interests. The conflict, compromise, or sometimes reconciliation of these interests was to be the main determinant of public policy, not the Hamiltonian ideal of a transcendant national interest, not the Rousseauan ideal of an overriding general will.

Here lay the heart of Hamilton's dilemma. As a genuine patriot of his adopted country, he was loyally committed to the practice of republican government. His grave doubts about the success of the experiment stemmed from his rejection of ethical individualism coupled with his acceptance of egoism as a fact of political life. The real trouble was that his end was incompatible with the means which, as a patriot, he had to accept. Logically, he should have ended up with some sort of philosopher-king theory, and he did have leanings in that direction. Since he was not a closet-philosopher, this way out of the dilemma was closed. There was really no way out. The way he chose, an alliance of one special interest group with what he conceived to be the national interest, simply stimulated opposition to the latter because he *had* linked it to the former. So he intensified in both groups the selfishness which was his enemy, and encouraged the growth of factions which he so deplored. That he was regarded by his contemporary opponents as a representative of class interests is perhaps regrettable, but their misunderstanding of him and his motives was no greater than his misunderstandnig of them and theirs. They were wrong in believing him to be an oligarch, but they were right in believing that his political ideals were opposed to theirs. His were corporate, theirs individualistic. His end was not logically anti-republican but, in the context of public opinion at the time, it was bound to make him doubtful that it could be achieved under republicanism. It was unlikely that the people, left to themselves, would faithfully pursue the national interest. They needed a Legislator. Hamilton volunteered for the job.

In this aspect of his thought—means rather than ends—I would again argue that Hamilton's ideas were subtly but profoundly different from those of most of his contemporaries. They all talked a lot about man's passions and emphasized the necessity of taking these into account when constructing a constitution. I think Hamilton had a much more ambitious opinion concerning the extent to which these passions could be actively used—manipulated—by politicians. Consider the benevolent passage quoted above in which he outlined the principles a wise politician must follow if he would lead the people toward the achievement of their happiness and the national interest. Consider his injunction that "it will ever be the duty of a wise government to avail itself of the passions, in order to make them subservient to the public good. . . ." Consider his proposal in the Convention to transfer sovereignty from the state governments to the national government in order to transfer the people's passions from the former to the latter. And consider his tendency during the 1790's to regard the people as dupes who had been led astray by designing politicians. All this adds up to a fairly consistent picture. The people are clay in the hands of the potter, but the potter may be either wise and virtuous, or shrewd and vicious. The former will give them what they ought to have, the latter will pretend to give them what they think they want.

As a Legislator, Hamilton was initially successful. The conditions which existed during and shortly after the inauguration of the new government were congenial for the exercise of his special talents. Afterwards, his effectiveness as politician and statesman declined with remarkable rapidity. Both his ends and his means were alien to the ideals and the experience of the people he sought to lead. Their ideals were liberal and individualistic, and their practice of self-government had rendered them impervious to the benevolent molding Hamilton had in mind to impose upon them. They would govern themselves. It was inevitable that he should be rejected.

Though his corporate idealism and manipulative methods be rejected, the central problem for which he offered them as solutions cannot be ignored. That problem is basic: how, in a nation governed by the people, is agreement on the public good to be obtained and put into effect? In this process, what is and should be the relationship between wisdom and public opinion, between private interest and national interest? These were fundamental questions when Hamilton grappled with them, and they still are. We have not yet worked out a satisfactory theory that will tell us precisely when the individual is ethically obligated to sacrifice his interests or when he may legitimately refuse to do so. Hamilton's plea for altruism in politics is relevant and salutary. The pursuit of selfish individual or group interests unrestrained by any sense of the general welfare may produce such bitter and divisive competition as to destroy the unity and consensus which sustain individual freedom as well as national strength.

Yet the Hamiltonian ideal, of each citizen placing the national interest before his own, is not without its dangers. It places an indefinite limitation on the exercise of individual freedom. There must be limits, of course, but this limit is an abstraction, and abstractions, when reified, are powerful forces to set against the solitary right and will of the individual. The national interest, with some exceptions such as sheer survival, will always be an elusive concept, its substance difficult to determine. Therefore there are practical reasons for refusing to concede it a permanently and categorically preferred position in all contests with individual, separate interests.

These practical reasons are merely corollaries of the main one. The main one is the ethical priority of the individual and his welfare as the proper and ultimate end of government. To this end, the national interest is logically and ethically secondary; to this end, the national interest must stand in the relationship of means. At least it must if one still accepts the Declaration of Independence as a statement of the purposes of American government. Hamilton mistook the means for

the end, and tipped the scale too far in the direction of the national interest. In so doing he gave it ethical priority over the demands of the individual.

Such a priority seems to necessitate resort to manipulative techniques in order to induce the individual to forego what he conceives to be his own interest. Thus Plato resorted to the persuasion of the myth of the metals, Rousseau to the authority of the gods. In his idealistic moods, Hamilton appealed to reason; in his self-consciously realistic moods, he attempted a calculated alliance between the national interest and selfish class interests. This was bound not only to accentuate conflict between factions, but to obscure the national interest itself. Hamilton's idealism was thus vitiated by a would-be realistic policy which was both shrewd and obtuse at the same time.

The fault lay in the man himself. Hamilton's idealism was genuine and profound. It was also touched with arrogance. His penchant for what he regarded as realism was a fundamental trait of his character; he liked to think of himself as a skillful maneuverer of men's emotions. Thus his realism was likewise touched with arrogance. It may be that this dual arrogance was subjectively justified—Hamilton *was* a superior individual. But in the politics of republican government, such arrogance may operate to blind its possessor to that which he must see and understand if he is to achieve a successful blend of idealism and realism. That is the nature of man, or, more specifically, the motivation and behavior of the voter. It was Hamilton's fortune to serve his country well for a brief and crucial period in its history; it was his fate to be rejected by the countrymen whose ideals he did not share, and whose politics he did not understand.

Alexander DeConde

WASHINGTON AS PRACTICAL POLITICIAN

Alexander DeConde's interpretation of Washington's supposedly apolitical Farewell Address emphasizes the partisan nature of that document. If Washington was at heart a pragmatic politician, perhaps all Federalists were motivated by political ambitions rather than ideals. According to DeConde, both the Federalists and Republicans were shrewd political observers whose objectives were practical and partisan. Could the same be said of their political beliefs: that these beliefs were grounded solely in pragmatic considerations? Was America's foreign policy primarily dictated by Federalist reaction against France's meddling in our domestic affairs, as DeConde maintains, or did the fear of entangling European alliances find its roots in more idealistic ground?

IN their conviction that the Federalist administration did not truly represent the American people, the French were encouraged by pro-French partisans among Republicans who indicated that the Federalist government would topple if only France were to take a strong stand. As the election year of 1796 opened, Republicans intensified their attacks against the Federalist administration. The Jay Treaty and the loud cry of aristocracy, monarchy, and plutocracy aroused deep popular emotions. Mutual hatred characterized the two large political segments of the American public.

With his government under fire on both domestic and foreign policy and with himself the target of unrestrained scurrility, Washington found the demands of his office increasingly difficult to endure. Publicly he maintained a dignified silence, but privately he revealed the strain. Even he had come to see that the myth of nonpartisanship was shattered, and that his concept of an administration above party and the tumult of politics had been illusory. Foreign relations had exploded the myth while serving as a catalyst in the formation of national political parties. This was an issue capable of transforming the opposing local alliances of Federalist and anti-Federalist into integrated national parties—an emotional foreign policy issue capable of capturing public imagination in a way which abstruse problems of finance could not.

Despite his increasing distaste for the office and the increasing speculation about his not wishing to be a candidate for a third term, the President remained silent as to future plans. Leaders of both political parties, however, had little doubt that he would not run. "He gave me intimations enough," asserted John Adams, "that his reign would be very short." Early in 1796, and even before, both parties had laid tentative plans which did not include Washington as a candidate.

The attacks on Washington grew increasingly bitter during the year. Opponents charged that he had betrayed a solemn pledge to France by destroying the French alliance. Personal attacks accused him of taking more salary than was allotted him. His mail was tampered with for political advantage, and forged letters of 1777 were refurbished and printed as genuine. Particularly cutting was Tom Paine's bitter attack from Paris, which city was the source, Federalists were convinced, of the anti-Washington campaign. Jefferson, too, had lost patience with the exalted role

From Alexander DeConde "Washington's Farewell Address, The French Alliance, and the Election of 1796," *Mississippi Valley Historical Review*, XLIII (March, 1957), pp. 646–50.

of Washington. The President, he wrote, like Samson had had his head "shorn by the harlot England."

Despite pressures to stay and ride out the storm, Washington disclosed in May, 1796, that he intended definitely to retire. If he had nurtured at all the desire to seek a third term it was killed by the acid criticism to which he had been subjected. The President decided not to seek a third term not only because he sought retirement in his old age but also because he was disgusted with the abuse from political opponents. "The true cause of the general's retiring," declared one of his staunchest supporters, "was . . . the *loss of popularity* which he had experienced, and the further loss which he apprehended from the rupture with France, which he looked upon as inevitable."

Once the decision to retire was made, Washington turned to Hamilton, as usual, for advice. When, he asked, would be the best time for publication of his farewell to the nation? Hamilton, with his eye on the coming election, advised that the public announcement be held off as long as possible. "The proper period now for your declaration," wrote Hamilton, "seems to be *Two months* before the time for the Meeting of the Electors. This will be sufficient. The parties will in the meantime electioneer conditionally, that is to say, *if you decline;* for a serious opposition to you will I think hardly be risked."

Three months before the gathering of electors Washington announced to the nation his intention to retire. Although in 1792 he had planned a valedictory to the nation and James Madison had drafted one, the September, 1796, version, in which Hamilton's hand was prominent, became a piece of partisan politics directed specifically against Republicans and Francophiles who had made Washington's last years miserable. At the time, it was recognized for what it was: a political manifesto, a campaign document. The 1792 version, drawn up before popular passions had been stirred by war in Europe, did not, for example, stress politics nor did it touch on foreign affairs. In the 1796 version partisan politics and foreign affairs were central.

Washington's specific target in foreign affairs, heartily seconded by Hamilton, was the alliance with France. He struck at Adet's partisan activities, at French meddling in American politics (while passing over British meddling), and at the allegedly dangerous implications of the French alliance. Washington told Hamilton that had it not been for the status of "party disputes" and of foreign affairs he would not have considered it necessary to revise his valedictory. He was convinced that a warning to the nation was necessary to combat foreign (French) intrigue "in the internal concerns of our country." It is indeed easy to "foresee," he warned, "that it may involve us in disputes and finally in War, to fulfill political alliances." This was the crux of the matter; Washington believed that the French alliance was no longer an asset to the country.

Washington's valedictory trumpeted the Federalist answer to Republican accusations that the administration had sold the country to the British; it countered the anti-administration furor over the Jay Treaty; it was a justification and defense of his policies. As such it was designed and as such it became the opening blast in the presidential campaign, contrived to prevent the election of Thomas Jefferson. The Farewell laid the basis for Federalist strategy of using Washington's great prestige to appeal to patriotism, as against the evil of foreign machinations, to make "Federalist" and "patriot" synonyms in the minds of the electorate. Under the banner of patriotism the Farewell spearheaded the attack on the opposition party and on French diplomacy.

In the address Washington opened with the announcement that he would not be a candidate for a third term and then stressed the advantages of union and the evils of political parties. Having in mind, undoubtedly, the French Republic, he advised against "a passionate attachment of one Nation for another."

Such "sympathy for the favourite nation," he warned, leads to wars and quarrels "without adequate inducement or justification." Then followed the oft-quoted "Great rule of conduct" that with foreign nations we should have "as little *political* connection as possible." While stressing fidelity to "already formed engagements," he announced that " 'tis our true policy to steer clear of permanent Alliances with any portion of the foreign world." Washington deplored the growth of political opposition, chastised the public for its attachment to France, and concluded with a defense of his foreign policy, particularly his much criticized policy of neutrality which was based on the Proclamation of April 22, 1793. He called this the "index" to his plan or policy.

Although cloaked in phrases of universal or timeless application, the objectives of the address were practical, immediate, and partisan. Men often attempt to rationalize their partisan political views in pronouncements studded with timeless patriotic appeals; so it was with Washington and Hamilton. The valedictory bore directly on the coming election, on the French alliance, and on the status of Franco-American relations in general.

While expressed cogently and linked forever with Washington's name, the main ideas and foreign policy principles of the Farewell were not unique with either Hamilton or Washington. They were prevalent Federalist ideas on current foreign policy and politics, and can be found expressed in various ways in the polemical literature of the time. The concept of no entanglement with Europe, for instance, was a common one among Federalists and others. More often than not it was a universalized reaction against a specific annoyance—the French alliance. Stated as non-involvement with Europe an attack against the alliance had great psychological appeal. In time this specific meaning was lost and only the generalization remained.

David H. Fischer

WASHINGTON AS IDEOLOGUE

David H. Fischer, an outstanding scholar of the younger generation of historians, presents the view that Washington was both an idealist and a politician. Fischer, like DeConde, sees Washington as a Federalist politician, but one whose actions were based upon principles. Washington believed in a corporate society in which there were inherent inequalities because all men tend to fall into one of two categories— the elite, or "discerning part of the community"; and the people, or "the lower class of citizens." For this reason Washington wanted a strong central government that could control "the people" by a combination of conciliation and repression.

AT first sight, Washington seems doubly irrelevant to this investigation of post-1800 Federalism, for he never called himself a Federalist and died in 1799. But on close inspection, there can be no doubt that he identified himself with the Federal Cause. In the last two years of his life, particularly, his disapproval of the Jeffersonian cause became intense. "You could as soon scrub a blackamore white, as to change the principles of a professt Democrat," he wrote angrily. He spoke of Federalists as "we" and Republicans as "they," broke completely with Thomas Jefferson himself, and threw his considerable weight behind Federal candidates in Virginia. His refusal to recognize the basic fact of his partisanship was typical of the old school. . . .

If Washington's physiognomy is familiar to all Americans, his political attitudes remain indistinct. He was, of course, no philosopher, but behind his acts and phrases was a set of attitudes which consistently embodied an "unspoken philosophy," as Douglas Southall Freeman has called it. At every important point, it was entirely compatible with the principles of his friends, George Cabot and John Jay. . . .

The fact is clear, though it may send a shudder through the serried ranks of the Daughters of the American Revolution, that Washington's social attitudes had a collectivist tinge. In place of Jefferson's notion of an individualized pursuit of happiness, Washington spoke of "the aggregate happiness of society, which . . . is, or ought to be, the end of all government." It was rare for him to use the libertarian language which has dominated American political rhetoric since 1800. Instead, he spoke and thought in terms of "the public good," the "interest of the commonwealth," the "benefit of the whole."

This corporate conception of society was, in Washington's mind, combined with a consciousness of inequalities among men. Like Cabot and Jay, he tended to divide men into the "discerning part of the community" on the one hand, and "the lower class of citizens" on the other. Though he believed that the people "mean well," he was never confident that they could resist the blandishments of "the discontented, the turbulent, the vicious." . . .

Washington was an elitist, but not a doctrinaire opponent of democracy. He firmly declared his allegiance to "the fundamental principle of our Constitution, which enjoins that the will of the majority shall prevail"—at the same time that he expressed a fear that "mankind, left to themselves, are unfit for their own government." These two sen-

From pp. 377–380 in *The Revolution of American Conservatism* by David Hackett Fischer. Copyright © 1965 by David Hackett Fischer. Reprinted by permission of Harper & Row, Publishers.

timents, though contradictory in our world, were compatible in Washington's. Their reconciliation lay in the deferential spirit of American society before the Revolution—a habitual subordination which was nowhere more evident than in Virginia. Even a French marquis noticed it. "The government may become democratic, as it is at the present moment," wrote Chastellux, "but the national character, the very spirit of the government, will always be aristocratic." . . .

Washington hoped that the people might possess sufficient wisdom to place their trust in "the virtuous and the wise" —to "choose able and honest representatives and leave them [free] in all national questions to determine from the evidence of reason, and the facts which shall be adduced." . . .

During the 1780s, he was deeply troubled by the course of public affairs in America. For him, at least, this controversial era was undeniably a critical period, but he diagnosed the crisis as moral rather than economic. "Virtue, I fear, has in great degree taken its departure from our land," he wrote to Jay. Ancient social habits, which from time immemorial had served as social cement were crumbling with astonishing speed. "If three years since," he wrote in 1787, "any person had told me . . . I should see such a formidable rebellion against the laws and Constitutions of our own making, as now appears, I should have thought him a bedlamite." . . .

His familiar reaction to Shays' rebellion was characteristic. "What, gracious God, is man! that there should be such inconsistency and perfidiousness in his conduct?" he wrote. Here was no unruffled observation on human nature, but the lamentation of a man who had temporarily lost both faith and hope. . . .

But the crisis of the 1780s did not disarm him altogether. Washington saw two remedies. First, a strong government, "a controulling power." To John Jay he wrote sadly, "We have errors to correct. We have probably had too good

an opinion of human nature in forming our confederation. Experience has taught us, that men will not adopt and carry into execution measures best calculated for their own good, without the intervention of a coercive power." One cannot know how far Washington wished to extend this "coercive power." During the fight for Jay's treaty he declared that "meetings in opposition to the constituted authorities" were "*at all times*, improper and dangerous." There was always a measure of the martial spirit in this soldier's social attitudes. . . .

But repression was never near the center of Washington's political thought. The "discontented, the turbulent, and the vicious" might be restrained by the "intervention of a coercive power," but Washington believed that it was "necessary to *conciliate* the good will of the people." To this purpose he prescribed the traditional American panacea, education. In his first annual Message to Congress, he spelled out his purpose— to teach the people "to distinguish between oppression and the necessary exercise of lawful authority, between burthens proceeding from a disregard to their convenience and those resulting from the inevitable exigencies of society, to discriminate the spirit of liberty from that of licentiousness." Not every American advocate of the common school has been driven by a faith in the common man. . . .

After 1799, Washington-worship assumed the proportions of a cult among the Federalists. There were political factors involved, of course. For partisan purposes, young Federalist party leaders made certain that Washington's "immortal shade" continued to haunt the Democrats, long after his mortal remains had been enshrined at Mount Vernon. But the reverence of the older Federalists cannot be dismissed as mere political posturing. If they made his life their measure of political morality, it was because he shared their assumptions and embodied their ideals.

Manning J. Dauer

REALISTS GUILTY OF FAULTY TACTICS

Manning J. Dauer believes that the political parties of the period were based on economic groupings; hence, in order to remain in power, the Federalists needed continued support of the commercial farmers. While John Adams was President, Dauer claims, he sought to keep commercial farmers within the Federalist party by maintaining moderate policies. When the Republicans began adopting many of the old Federalist policies, however, the more extreme Hamiltonian Federalists transformed their party into an instrument for the financial and shipping interests. Without the support of the commercial farmers, the Federalists lost power and soon disappeared as a viable, national political party. It was the extreme Federalists, Dauer concludes, not the Adams Federalists, who were responsible for the decline of the party after 1797. If the Federalists were realists, why did they fail to understand the necessity for retaining the swing vote of the commercial farmers—the crucial third force in American politics of the period?

HOW and why did American political parties begin? During the period before the Revolution, divisions appeared. The colonial period was full of political conflicts within each colony. On the eve of the Revolution, the division of Whig versus Tory developed in every colony, and Whigs and Tories alike united among the colonies. During the Revolution, this division passed beyond the political level to the level of civil war. But by the end of the Revolution, in 1783, the Tories had either migrated or been suppressed. Soon, however, a new division appeared—Federalist versus Anti-Federalist. Should the thirteen states unite in a stronger form of government, or retain the weak union of a confederation?

Although political parties fought over the issue of adopting the new constitution which established a federal form of government, their continuation on a national basis and their role in the government were not fully foreseen by the makers of the Constitution. Nor do writers on parties of this period more than partially understand their role. The ideas held by Hamilton, Madison, and Jay as expressed in *The Federalist* are not so discerning on this subject as on others. There was discussion of "Factions" and the influence these would have. But the assumption was that any factions, or political parties, would be local or regional. It was foreseen that there would be continuing differences among social, economic, and geographic groups; but how these would be expressed was a speculative matter.

*   *   *

While in New England the decentralization of the shipbuilding industries makes the calculation of the extent of agricultural *versus* commercial sections difficult, it is doubtful if even in this section the direct mercantile interests had sufficient votes to carry a single state. Even in New England in 1800 it is estimated that, of a total population of 1,078,546, the population of commercial towns came only to about 145,000. John A. Krout and Dixon Ryan Fox state that during the period around 1800 "at least nine Americans out of ten, even in commercial New England, dug their

From Manning Dauer, *The Adams Federalists* (Baltimore, 1953), pp. 1–7, 262–265. Reprinted by permission of Johns Hopkins Press.

living from the land." This statement is indisputable for the country as a whole; but because of the importance of shipping, shipbuilding, and the fisheries, it is probably an overstatement for much of New England and especially for eastern New England. But it serves to point up the political problem generally. Any political party which wished to maintain a majority had to secure considerable agrarian support.

On the other hand, Alexander Hamtilton's policy was the basis of the Federalist party program. Initially, in 1790, his program of a strong central government commanded fairly broad support. Washington, as president, became the symbol of this policy. But opposition to a strong central government already had arisen over the adoption of the Constitution. While this opposition somewhat disintegrated as the new government started, it soon reappeared. As Beard has shown in his *Economic Origins of Jeffersonian Democracy,* the basis of the Jeffersonian Republican party's strength was agrarian. With the United States so strongly agrarian, why, then, did the Jeffersonian party not become successful upon the retirement of Washington in the presidential contest of 1796?

There are a variety of reasons for this. But one of the central ones is the support of the Federalist party by agricultural sections throughout the country. This is also the explanation of John Adams' strength in the Federalist party. By centering attention on the Adams supporters, instead of on the Hamilton supporters, it becomes apparent that the history of the decline of the Federalist party is largely the history of the step-by-step loss of the agrarian elements from the party. It also becomes apparent that religious and cultural factors influenced the extent to which agrarian elements tied in with Federalism or Jeffersonian Republicanism. . . . In most states the general pattern is that the more self-sufficient farming sections and the "mechanic interests" of the cities are the centers of Jeffersonian strength. The extreme Federalists are found among the commercial

and shipping sections, and the exporting agricultural sections are somewhat less intensely Federalist. . . .

The soundness of the position taken by Charles A. Beard, that the Federalist policy favored the commercial groups, while the Republicans represented the agrarians, is accepted as fundamental. However, although this is true of the Federalist *policy;* yet Federalist *support* was derived from a broader basis. In general, the Half-Federalists, as those who deviated from Hamiltonian orthodoxy are called, are to be found in farming sections. . . .

*   *   *

. . . Organized national political parties were not fully foreseen. Washington launched his administration under such a conception of the presidency, appointing his heads of departments from all factions, including both Jefferson and Hamilton in the original group. But before his second administration closed, this theory had been abandoned of necessity. His cabinet was a Federalist cabinet. The party was headed by Hamilton, even though Hamilton had left the cabinet for New York.

The trend in this direction is perfectly clear in the party press of the period. The *Aurora,* national organ of the Republicans, hailed Washington's retirement with delight. In 1799, when Washington was urged to run for a third term, among reasons he gave for declining was that he clearly saw the growth of parties had prevented universal acceptance of the President. The country would be no more united under him than under some other president, he maintained.

Adams was not as clear on the connection which had developed between the presidency and the parties by 1799 as was Washington. He still hoped, throughout his administration, for the President to be regarded as above party, as representing the national interest. At the same time, he sometimes acted on the opposite theory, that he needed to take steps to build a party interest around himself. This becomes the impression when one considers part of his plans and his relationship to Elbridge Gerry, Benjamin Rush, the Muhlenbergs, the Fenners, and others. Here he seemed to be trying to build a faction or party of his own, or to take over the Federalist party himself. But in the main, Adams acted on his theory of the independent executive.

The force which actually proved strongest in the development of American politics was the growth of parties. The authority of the President rested upon political power as represented by these parties. The question next arises, why did these parties grow up? The answer is found in terms of the economic, social, religious, cultural, and geographic influences of the period. These factors divided the people into divergent groups. These groups coalesced into two major combinations—the commercial (Federalist) and the agrarian (Republican). But the economic elements named are merely those which dominated in each party. A considerable portion of farmers who grew cash crops supported the Federalists until 1800 or shortly thereafter. Artisans in the cities were generally Republican. But once a stable central government was established, the dominance of agriculture in the American economy assured that the Jeffersonians would triumph if they could develop a moderate program. They did so. They drew off the middle class of farmers from the Federalists. They modified sufficiently their opposition to banks to assure a banking program for the expanding economy of the country. In contrast, Federalist policy, while ambitious, was designed increasingly for commercial groups alone. Except where some extraordinary factor like the Congregational Church entered, as it did in the state of Connecticut, this program was too extreme to hold the farm support to the party. The result was the split in policy in 1799–1800, peace with France, the election of Jefferson, the ultimate extinction of the Federalist party.

There is another matter of importance. With the growth of political parties an important extension of the principles of free speech and free press occurred. The idea of an opposition political party having the right to exist had necessarily received a set-back because of the strife between Whigs and Tories during the American Revolution. Civil war at home accompanied the war with England. With the growth of political parties under the new constitution there were two immediate dangers after 1789. One was that organized political parties might not be granted the right to exist. This danger was typified by the Alien and Sedition Laws. The other danger was that the splitting off process of the American Revolution might be continued, perhaps through the program possibly suggested by the Virginia and Kentucky Resolutions, or the secession plans of the extreme Federalists for New England.

But the constitutional government established, through the medium of political parties, proved capable of bringing the divergent groups representing political power into an adjustment with one another that was acceptable to the great majority. This was achieved through the legislative process. Protest and change came through the electoral process. To some degree Adams contributed to this. But his major contribution was probably not ideological, not his idea of an independent executive and a balance. His major contribution, instead, was made because he thought with the moderates. It was in that way that his great decision—peace with France, no foreign adventure, an end to domestic extremism—contributed greatly to the development of ultimate national well-being. He also contributed to the establishment of a peaceful method whereby change could take place within the framework of constitutional republican government, which ultimately became democratic government.

A question may be raised concerning the political leadership exercised by Adams. It has already been suggested that Jefferson came close, after his inaugural, to moulding together the rather disparate groups which had opposed extreme Federalist policy. Had it been possible for Adams to follow, from 1797 on, the policy which he did after his break with the cabinet, he might have had a comparable reception. Honesty and forthrightness he had in abundance. He was motivated by an intense sense of trusteeship on behalf of his countrymen. In this respect he sought, like Washington, to be impartial. He stood against the extremists of his own party. But, impetuous in temperament, he lacked the ability of great political leaders like Jefferson and Lincoln to carry with him the groups necessary to political success.

Lawrence S. Kaplan

IDEOLOGUES WHO COMMITTED POLITICAL SUICIDE

Lawrence S. Kaplan differs sharply with Dauer regarding the reasons for the Federalist defeat in the election of 1800. The Federalists, according to Kaplan, were rigid ideologues who refused to change with the temper of the times. By their stubborn refusal to become more flexible, the Federalists committed "political suicide." Did the Federalists knowingly maintain unpopular policies, or did they expect to be recalled to power after the Republicans had failed in office? Was it possible that the Federalists might have remained politically alive had they changed their tactics?

FEW groups in American history have been treated more severely than the Federalist party of the last decade of the eighteenth century. The original charges of intellectual arrogance, social snobbery, and economic bias have defied periodic conservative attempts to hail an Alexander Hamilton, if not a Timothy Pickering, as a lodestar of America's destiny. Even the post-World War II reconstruction of the Founding Fathers, among whom Federalists predominate, has failed to create a favorable national image of Federalism. If a particular Federalist is momentarily revived through publication of his papers, his party role is usually minimized. The party itself stalks through the pages of American history as a deviant from American democracy.

Among questions worth asking about the Federalists is whether they were guilty as charged. What kind of men were they, and what kind of America did they envisage for themselves and their posterity? If their universe was truly confined to the rich and well-born, did Hamilton's adroitness, in general, and his manipulation of a bogus French menace, in particular, explain their decade of power? Or did they have appeal to a wider constituency? In their last years the un-American qualities of the party seemed accentuated by their Anglophilism. Yet, few scholars have fully addressed themselves to the question whether they represented a faction tied to the former mother country by bonds of commerce and social aspirations, or were enlightened internationalists believing that the future of America and of civilization was linked to the survival of Great Britain in the war against the French Revolution. Lastly, did Jefferson's election in 1800 represent a national repudiation of an obsolescent party or a factional split caused by faulty political tactics and sharp personal antagonisms?

Rather than dwell upon the Essex Junto, that embittered little band of Massachusetts sectionalists who have left their stamp upon the party image, one more appropriately might begin with the victorious Federalists of 1790, fresh from constructing a Constitution and in the process of creating a new government. They knew what they wanted after the fever years of the Confederation. It was a society that would preserve the social order first threatened by British imperialism a generation before and then by western democracy in the past decade. Government and society should remain in the hands of those best equipped to control them, and the Constitution was their instrument to keep their world in proper check and balance.

Federalist attachment to traditional mores, fear of emotional outbursts from

Reprinted with permission from Lawrence S. Kaplan's "The Decline and Fall of Federalism: Historical Necessity?" in Quint, Albertson and Cantor, eds., *Main Problems in American History*, 1964 edition, Vol. I (Homewood, Ill.: The Dorsey Press) pp. 106–116.

the populace, concern for maintenance of established institutions all suggest an analogue to Europe's *ancien régimes* that is probably unwittingly reinforced among scholars by the passion of Federalist denunciation of the French Revolution abroad and the "Jacobins" at home. Yet the Federalists have as much right to be identified with the brave new world of revolution as any Republican and more than most European revolutionaries. Federalists both produced and were a product of a Constitution which assumed that government originated in a social contract and would be best managed in a republican form built around the consent of the governed. Power might be curbed or channeled to offset the dangers of popular democracy, but the Federalists never had any doubt about the proper source of power. Commissioned to perform emergency services as well as to design long-term governmental arrangements, they spoke for an entire nation, not just for one or two privileged estates.

If the nation was to survive, it had to assure its people that the centrifugal forces of state governments could be and would be curbed. If the nation was to prosper, it had to create a fiscal program that would repay the long-standing debts to domestic and foreign creditors and provide a firm basis for the expansion of the economy. If the nation was to expand, it had to inform the world that its government could protect its territories from attack and pursue opportunities for acquisition of new territories when they appeared. The Constitution and the branches of government it established made these activities possible; Hamilton was largely responsible for making them successful.

The result was that in the first years of the federal republic, Federalism was a movement rather than a faction shared in one way or another by the entire country. Just as Washington could be elected and re-elected without opposition, so a Jefferson and a Hamilton could sit together in his Cabinet. In the Congress Madison of Virginia might be joined by Rufus King of New York on more issues than might separate them; if they disagreed, the differences initially were not particularly ideological or partisan. Frontier farmers west of the Appalachians could look upon the federal government with favor as a source of protection from Indian attack and British or Spanish intimidation. It is unlikely that their expectations were any less selfish or less sanguine than were those of eastern speculators awaiting the government's assumption of hitherto valueless securities. For a group which has been identified with pessimism and reaction, the buoyant optimism present in much of Washington's first administration was remarkably American, if un-Federalist.

In retrospect, the student can easily locate the elements within Federalism that would rapidly lead to schismatic class and regional conflicts. While Hamilton's blueprint for America's future—clearly etched in his monumental reports as Secretary of the Treasury—could be justified in the name of the national interest, the most immediate benefits would fall to certain people rather than to all. Such men represented definable groups—commercial, wealthy, educated—in definable geographical areas—urban, eastern, maritime. Hamilton not only understood the implications of unfair distribution of advantages but ardently sought to use them for the benefit of the country as he saw it. The beneficiaries of his program were the very people whose support of the new federal Union was most needed. Without seeking personal profit, he facilitated special dividends for prominent friends through judicious distribution of stock in the Bank of the United States, the corporation chartered by the Congress and supplied with funds from the federal Treasury. It would have been difficult for a financier to find a more prudent investment.

In all his actions, consideration for the economic interests of the small farmer, who comprised the vast majority of the population, was intentionally absent. Agrarian society, with its democratic bias, would not produce the kind of America Hamilton envisaged. Instead, there would be a static population, limitations upon the production of wealth, and the denigration of intellectual and cultural distinction. Even if the farmer had been favored by government measures, would he have been farsighted enough to utilize them? Hamilton thought not. The farmer was to pay for his program through excise taxes (on such items as whisky); and the resultant Whisky Rebellion of 1794 represented a protest against a system of taxation designed to make those *least able to pay* produce revenue that would serve those *most able to pay*.

As a consequence of these bold discriminatory policies, it is not surprising to find an organized opposition rising against Federalism. Urban laborers, southerners, westerners, and farmers everywhere had reason to complain. More than economic self-interest united them. Under the banner of democracy, Jefferson and the former Federalist, Madison, could condemn Hamiltonian Federalism as a betrayal of the principles of the American Revolution. Madison, in Congress, railed against inequity in the funding and assumption bills; he found them unfair to the original holder of public securities—the little man who had sold his worthless paper to the speculator and consequently gained nothing from federal action. Hamilton's answer: "A relaxation of this kind would tend to dissolve all social obligations—to render all rights precarious, and to introduce a general dissoluteness and corruption of morals." Jefferson, in the Cabinet, pointed with even more vehemence to the dangers which the creation of the Bank of the United States would have for states' rights under the Constitution. Hamilton retorted with the doctrine of implied powers: "If the end be clearly comprehended within any of the specified powers, and if the measure have an obvious relation to that end, and is not forbidden by any particular provision of the Constitution, it may safely be deemed to come within the compass of the national authority." Hamilton's arguments and personality won out on both counts, but at a high price: The Federalists, men who deplored faction, were responsible for

establishing a dissenting bloc, the Anti-Federalists, out of which the Republican party emerged.

For Republicans, the most dangerous and most vulnerable aspect of Federalism lay in its resolute Anglophilism, which was expressed not only in its bias in favor of the commercial interests but also in its excessive admiration for the social system of monarchy. The latter issue was brought to a head with the opening of the French revolutionary wars in 1793. Jefferson regarded the occasion as one when Americans should support republicanism as well as the cause of a valued friend who had helped the United States win its freedom. European conflict at the same time inflamed popular Anglophobia, which was regularly nourished by the continuing British presence in the Northwest posts, contrary to the Treaty of Paris. To this irritant was added the impressment of American seamen into British warships, the seizure of French goods from American vessels, and a definition of contraband that violated the American conception of neutral rights.

Federalist reaction to the European war could have played into the hands of the opposition, but the Washington administration refused to bow to popular emotions. On the contrary, friendship with Britain became more important than ever. Until 1793, Great Britain had been the motherland, the country whose society was worthy of emulation and whose errors had made separation necessary, if regrettable. More critically, Britain was the commercial and industrial leader of the world, to whom American prosperity was geared by the machinery of credit and supplies. After 1793, however, Britain's significance was ideological as well as social and economic. Its defeat at the hands of France would be the destruction of civilization itself. Should the British succumb to French Jacobinism, the United States would fall victim to its American counterpart.

As the Federalists saw it, the United States had to support Great Britain for its own survival, and no Francophilic sentiment should be allowed to deflect such assistance. Hamilton attempted to use his influence in the Cabinet to denounce the Franco-American alliance of 1778 and, failing this, to hinder French attempts to use American port facilities for disposal of prizes and arming of warships. The foolish behavior of Edmond Genêt, the youthful French minister, in speaking out against the President permitted him partial success. To forestall what probably would have been a successful Republican attempt to impose a nonintercourse act against Britain, Hamilton managed to have Chief Justice John Jay sent to London in 1794 to settle the differences between the two countries.

Jay's Treaty resulted. Along with it came such a storm of protest against the Federalists and the British that Jay was burned in effigy in Philadelphia and Hamilton stoned in the streets of New York. The latter's fate might have been even worse had Republican mobs known that he had induced the British minister to the United States to disregard American threats of joining a league of European armed neutrals in the event Britain refused to meet American demands on the high seas. In effect, Jay had renounced the freedom of the seas, proclaimed jointly with France in 1778, by permitting the British to remove enemy goods from American ships. British concessions by comparison appeared unimpressive, if indeed the long-delayed evacuation of western fur posts and the official establishment of commercial relations may properly have been considered concessions.

The wonder in this treaty and in the Federalist responsibility for its passage in the Senate is that Federalism was not thoroughly repudiated at the polls a little over a year later when Washington's second term in office expired. Yet the Federalists, not the Jeffersonian Republicans, won the presidential election. If the Federalists were in jeopardy in 1796, it was less because of a shameful betrayal to Britain than because of an equally shameful internal feud between Hamilton and the presidential candidate, John Adams.

What do the election results tell, then, about the first eight years of Federalist administration? They might suggest national satisfaction with a government which had set up an efficient civil service with standards rarely matched in later generations. Or they might represent approval of a government which had solved fiscal instability with the Bank of the United States and had ironed out the troubles of interstate commerce. Foreign wars brought prosperity to American commerce and agriculture. Not even the excess energy displayed by Hamilton in suppressing the whisky rebels of Pennsylvania could convince the nation that the price of vigorous government was the loss of personal liberty. More likely, such actions impressed the nation favorably by showing that the administration could surmount crises that would have defeated the Confederation. And when the heat had gone from Jay's Treaty, westerners could take satisfaction in Britain's evacuation of the Northwest Territory and Spain's opening of the port of New Orleans to American commerce. Although the concession of right of deposit was the product of Pinckney's Treaty in 1795, it may be claimed that Pinckney might not have had such favorable terms had the Spanish not been afraid that Jay's Treaty presaged an Anglo-American alliance or, at least, an anti-Spanish alliance.

Whether the voter, absorbed with local issues and local prejudices, ever recognized by his electoral ballot the full measure of Federalist services to the republic is impossible to gauge. It is fair to assert, however, that the charges of monarchism and Anglophilism left over from Jay's Treaty were not campaign issues, as the Jeffersonians had anticipated. Rather, there were the words of the retiring President, an embittered figure caught up in the rising partisanship of his second administration: Washington's farewell address warned his countrymen against the dangers of foreign attachments, and in his mind the ties and the nation he feared were France, not England.

Assuming the role of an injured party as a result of Jay's Treaty, the French Directory meddled in the internal affairs of the United States at a most unpropitious moment for Republican fortunes. Its activities blunted American resentment against England much as Genêt's prating had diverted attention from British annoyances in 1793. After failing to defeat the treaty in the Senate by making known its legitimate if not legal grievances against the United States, France attempted to have it revoked by supporting Jefferson's election to the presidency in 1796. Such brazen intervention in American politics lost for the Republicans whatever advantage they might have derived from the unpopularity of Federalist Anglophilism. John Adams and Federalism survived the election of 1796 by three electoral votes.

But the miseries of office about which President Washington had complained so bitterly in his last years now spread to include all Federalists. Preferring the more pliant Thomas Pinckney to the independent Adams as Washington's successor, Hamilton nearly had managed to have his way. This intraparty dispute—in which the rivalry of Hamilton and Adams almost cost the latter the election of 1796—now cast its shadow over the next four years. Based in part on personality differences and deepened by the enormous power Hamilton had been accustomed to wielding in or out of office, it led ultimately to defeat at the polls in 1800. And what might have been a temporary setback, in turn, exposed fatal flaws in Federalism which previously had been buried by success.

The besetting weakness of the Federalists as divisions among them unfolded after 1797 was fear of all kinds stemming from their baleful outlook on the world. Fears of atheism, anarchy, and Thomas Jefferson increasingly dominated their thoughts and actions. What triggered these fears in 1797 was the special terror of France, an angry vengeful France that had begun to punish America for its friendship with England

by seizing vessels and confiscating cargo without compensation—and with less excuse than the British. Federalists became convinced of what they had only suspected earlier, namely, that France's hostility was part of a master plan of world conquest in which the United States would join Britain as victim of the French Revolution. They were equally convinced that the Jeffersonians were agents of France in achieving this objective.

Ironically, the first move of the Adams administration might have kept these fears in check and Hamilton's influence under control had France displayed suitable tact. The President, following the Jay precedent, decided upon a conciliatory mission to France composed of two Federalists and one Republican. In fact, Hamilton had been willing to include Jefferson as the Republican delegate had the Vice President not declined the invitation.

The mission failed disastrously. The Directory refused to meet the Americans without a bribe for the foreign minister, a loan to the government, and apologies for American's hostile behavior of the past few years. Publication of the "negotiation" with X, Y, and Z—Talleyrand's agents in 1798—combined with the peremptory American rejection of these terms, raised Federalism to a pinnacle of what proved to be an illusory success. Indeed, its very success, as reflected in the war mood of a now Francophobic America, led to the party's undoing.

Repression of political enemies and sharpened internal divisions marked the future course of Federalism as it embarked on an unofficial naval war with France. The prospect of war immediately aroused Federalists to an increased awareness of danger within the body politic in the form of Republicanism, the putative puppet of France. Since Congress had to cope with the enemy abroad by repudiating treaties of commerce and alliance, by raising money for ships and men, and by conducting warfare on the high seas, surely it should deal with equal vigor against the enemy at home; at least, so thought the administration. Consequently, but somewhat uncharacteristically, John Adams allowed himself to be carried away by war fervor to the point of recommending to the nation a series of laws designed as counterparts to military action. They are popularly known as the Alien and Sedition acts of 1798, and have become affixed to the name of Federalism over the years as a badge of its repressive intentions.

The political uses of the alien and the naturalization laws were obvious. If the President had the power to deport undesirable aliens and could extend the process of naturalization from five to fourteen years, he could delay and discourage potential Republican voters from Ireland from casting ballots against Federalists. The fear that inspired this Act also was responsible for another measure—the Sedition Act— that was even more broadly political and psychopathic in motivation, and that had less of a constitutional basis; after all, the powers invoked under the naturalization law were those inherent in a nation's sovereignty.

The Sedition Act provided heavy fines and imprisonment for those judged guilty of writing or speaking against the government—the President or Congress —when such utterances might be considered scandalous or malicious. Modeled after the English common law of seditious libel, the Sedition Act was an improvement over British internal security legislation. According to Professor Mark DeWolfe Howe, it eliminated "those elements in English law to which objections had been persistently made on both sides of the Atlantic during the eighteenth century." Nevertheless, the law hardly squared with the guarantees of the First Amendment. It aimed a clearly directed blow at domestic political opposition; it was animated by hostility to criticism and equated dissent with treason; it sought, in the words of a leading Federalist senator, Robert Harper, to "equally resist our external enemies and domestic traitors."

How bad was the ensuing "reign of terror"? Only one section of the measure was enforced; only a few editors were convicted under its provisions; and none of them were trundled off to the guillotine. Indeed, the Act may be found more disgraceful than destructive. It heightened the anti-Federalist attack and was partly responsible for the substantial growth of opposition newspapers. The widely publicized Kentucky and Virginia resolutions, written secretly by Jefferson and Madison out of fear of imminent arrest, also aroused criticism of the party in power (though, it might be added, the Republicans were not sure that state interposition was the answer to their problems). The fact of a free election in which Jefferson himself emerged the victor also raises doubts about the extent and effectiveness of the Federalist frenzy.

The tragedy of the repressive and impolitic Sedition Act for Federalists was the exposure of the misanthropy that underlay their behavior. It was not a pleasant sight. Americans generally could not accept the Federalist equation of Republicans with French Jacobinism, let alone with Satan's minions about to unleash destruction upon the good works of the past decade. Adams succumbed to this malaise only periodically, but many of his colleagues never recovered from it. This outlook contributed materially to the party's destruction by interpreting all events since 1798 as a fulfillment of Federalist predictions of doom.

Although, in 1798 and 1799, the overseas enemy often appeared less an issue than the domestic struggle, the French imbroglio served to reopen the feud between the President and Hamilton. The latter now sought a military power, second only to Washington's, as he realized the opportunities a war with France would have for cementing Anglo-American relations and for winning fresh personal laurels as a military chieftain. Not least of Hamilton's rewards would be the elimination of Republicanism as the party of treason. John Adams destroyed most of these dreams by giving him the uniform—and little more. Just as the Sedition Act had pandered to the President's vanity, so the bold demands of Hamilton touched his pride. Had he acceded to a formal war with France, he would have surely ended his term as Hamilton's figurehead, heading a Cabinet that looked to New York for leadership.

But it was more than jealousy that led Adams to seek *rapprochement* with France. His conception of the national interest, which was that of all Federalists in their sober moments, was the independence from Europe articulated by Washington in 1796. War with France would push America into Europe's maelstrom and endanger all that had been accomplished since the framing of the Constitution as surely as would Jefferson's control of the government. Was not this Hamilton's own opinion in 1797? Reports from Europe convinced Adams that Talleyrand had regretted his highhanded behavior toward the American mission and would receive a new emissary with proper respect. Hamilton and his Cabinet friends strenuously opposed the idea but succeeded only to the extent of expanding the size of the mission to what they hoped would be the fatal number of three. Leaving aside the devious motives of the new French Consulate for an accommodation with the United States, no critic would deny major credit for the Convention of Mortefontaine in 1800 to the doggedness of Adams in overruling the Hamiltonians.

Adams was repaid for his services to the country by defeat in 1800, largely at the hands of his own party. Having discharged most of his Cabinet in the spring of that year for personal disloyalty over the issue of the mission to France, the President had invited the wrath of Hamilton, who attempted to replace him with another Pinckney, this time Charles Cotesworth rather than his brother Thomas. Hence, Thomas Jefferson reversed the verdict of 1796 with the unintended help of his avowed enemy Hamilton.

Did the election results signify a national rejection of the incumbent party? Federalism's narrow defeat suggests nothing of the sort. True, the country was stirred to a degree by the passions of the Kentucky resolutions. Undeniably, the Federalist war taxes were unpopular. On the other hand, Adams was shown to be more popular than he had been in 1796. And deservedly so. His action had spared the country war and released it from the entangling alliances with France. But the split within the Federalist ranks blurred the image of a party that offered everything the country would support in 1800—or in 1804—peace with Europe, stable government, and commercial expansion.

Hamilton's romantic ambitions, however, stripped the veil from the mortal failing of the Federalists: their propensity for self-destruction. It was hardly their rejection of democracy that defeated them; many Republicans shared this attitude. Their demise stemmed from a refusal to accept the responsibilities of politics in America, the ability to concede some objectives to win others. Had they not grown so ideologically rigid by 1800, they might have returned to power in 1804 or in 1808. Any party proclaiming Federalist principles that could win three successive presidential elections should certainly hope to win another in the immediate future. Their apocalyptic vision of America in 1800 and afterward doomed them more than the personality conflicts within the party itself. They could not or would not even recognize that Jefferson's administration was little more than a refinement of the government they had created. Had Republicanism genuinely defeated Federalism, Federalists today might have enjoyed the favor Americans often give to battlers for lost causes. By turning their backs on their country and their swords on themselves, they merit the special reputation Americans give to suicides.

SUGGESTIONS FOR ADDITIONAL READING

The best bibliographical introductions to the historical literature of the period may be found in Stephen G. Kurtz, *Presidency of John Adams* (Philadelphia, 1957); John C. Miller, *The Federalist Era, 1789–1801* (New York, 1960); and Keith B. Berwick, *The Federal Age, 1789–1829* (Washington, 1961). For an overview of the decade when the Federalists were in power from two different perspectives, three articles will prove profitable to the student. Marshall Smelser's "The Jacobin Phrenzy: Federalism and the Menace of Liberty, Equality, and Fraternity," *The Review of Politics*, XIII (October, 1951), 457–482, and his "The Jacobin Phrenzy: The Menace of Monarchy, Plutocracy, and Anglophobia, 1789–1798," *The Review of Politics*, XXI (January, 1959), 239–258; and John R. Howe's "Republican Thought and the Political Violence of the 1790's" *American Quarterly*, XIV (Summer, 1967), pp. 147–165.

Most general works about the Federalists prior to World War II were characterized by extreme partisanship. Scholars writing about the Federalist era invariably identified themselves with either Hamilton or Jefferson. In fact, many scholars tended to view all of American history in terms of a Hamiltonian-Jeffersonian dichotomy and to look upon the Federalist period as providing the key to the rest of the nation's political history.

Even general histories of the period written after World War II betray a pro-Hamilton or pro-Jefferson bias, though often to a less marked degree. John C. Miller's, *The Federalist Era,* the most balanced synthesis of the decade when the Federalists were in power, is guardedly pro-Hamiltonian. Nathan Schachner's, *The Founding Fathers* (New York, 1954), is quite pronounced in its pro-Hamiltonian point of view. Joseph C. Charles' more specialized study, *Origins of the American Party System* (Williamsburg, 1956), on the other hand, is as critical of the Federalists as any contemporary Jeffersonian Republican.

Marcus Cunliffe in *The Nation Takes Shape, 1789–1837* (Chicago, 1959), holds that by concentrating on the decade when the Federalists were in power, historians have placed undue emphasis upon "periodization" and have missed the point that the American national character emerged over a longer period of time—the first half-century of the nation's life.

Moving back in time, one can trace the rise of a pro-Federalist and pro-Jeffersonian interpretation of the period. During the first three-quarters of the 19th century, the majority of American historians took what might be termed a Federalist-Whig-Republican point of view rather than a Jeffersonian-Jacksonian-Democratic outlook. Typical of this approach was Richard Hildreth's six-volume *History of the United States* (Boston, 1849–52), in which the author, a Massachusetts Whig, took a friendly view of the Federalists and had high praise for Hamilton. The brilliant nine-volume study by Henry Adams, *The History of the United States during the Administrations of Jefferson and Madison* (New York, 1889–1891), remains the classic work on the Federalists after 1801, and one of the monumental contributions to American scholarship. Although his history could not be considered pro-Jeffersonian, Adams was openly hostile to the Federalist party which had rejected his great-grandfather, John Adams; he concluded that the Federalist leaders were conservative and decadent figures in an American society that was essentially dynamic and democratic.

Around the turn of the century, the majority of American historians began viewing the nation's past from a Jeffersonian-Jacksonian-Democratic perspective for the first time. Three scholars working within the Progressive historiographical tradition—Charles A. Beard, Claude G. Bowers, and Vernon L. Parrington—began rewriting the history of the Federalist period from the vantage point of Jeffersonian democracy. Beard in his *Economic Origins of Jeffersonian Democracy* (New York, 1915), pointed out that the Federalists helped bring about their own defeat by passing unpopular legislation—Jay's Treaty, the Sedition Act, and direct taxes. Bowers' book, *Jefferson and Hamilton* (New York, 1925), pictured the Federalist decade as a struggle between the democratic and anti-democratic forces with Jefferson's election signifying the triumph of democracy. Vernon L. Parrington in his three-volume work, *Main Currents in American Thought* (New York, 1927), pictured Jefferson as the philosopher of agrarian democracy. To Parrington the major theme in American thought was the enduring dichotomy throughout the nation's history between two rival political philosophies—the liberal and idealistic tradition of Jefferson and the conservative and materialistic one personified by Hamilton. Parrington had no problem deciding where his sympathies lay; he admitted his bias was "liberal rather than conservative, Jeffersonian rather than Federalistic." These three scholars saw all of American history—including the Federalist period—in terms of conflict and disunity; as a series of clashes between the rich and poor, conservatives and liberals, and democratic versus undemocratic forces.

Since World War II, the trend has been away from the extreme partisanship characteristic of most earlier scholars of the period. The rise of a group of so-called "consensus historians" led to placing greater emphasis upon the broad areas of agreement between the Federalists and Republicans rather than upon the disagreements that divided them. The ideas of all America's political leaders were considered as being more similar than dissimilar because of their common acceptance of the basic concepts of the Enlightenment—reason, experience, and progress—hence resulting in a consensus. Men pictured in the past as being at opposite poles in political and ideological terms were now seen as sharing the same basic political philosophy. Richard Hofstadter's discussion of the Federalists in his *American Political Tradition and the Men Who Made It* (New York, 1948), represents the consensus point of view which has revised the position taken by the Progressive historians who emphasized conflict. Some commentators suggested that the rise of the "consensus historians" evidenced America's newfound conservatism as the United States emerged as a world leader in the postwar era: that scholars, either consciously or subconsciously, reflected a concern for national security by stressing the theme of consensus among the American people throughout their history in order to present the image of a nation that was strong and united to the rest of the world.

The Federalist position has been analyzed in a number of recent studies. Zoltan Haraszti in his *John Adams and the Prophets of Progress* (Cambridge, 1952), has provided the most illuminating insights into the Federalist mind and shown the richness of political thought that lay behind Adams' actions. The best statement of the neo-Beardian point of view of the Federalists is Manning J. Dauer's *The Adams Federalists* (Baltimore, 1953). Stephen G. Kurtz has the most comprehensive account of the Adams administration and a good analysis of how the President dealt with his problems. The finest study of the Federalists from 1800–1816 is David H. Fischer's *Revolution of American Conservatism* (New York, 1965). Shaw Livermore in his *Twilight of Federalism* (Princeton, 1962), has shown that the Federalists were politically active long after the party supposedly disappeared from the scene in 1816. A minor classic and still very valuable is Dixon Ryan Fox's older work, *Decline of Aristocracy in the Politics of New York, 1801–1840* (New York, 1918), which is a case study of what happened to the Federalists on the state level after the defeat in the national election of 1800.

Federalist leadership has been perceptively examined in a few key articles in recent years. The most searching study of the social and political attitudes of the Massachusetts Federalist leaders is in David H. Fischer's "The Myth of the Essex Junto," *William and Mary Quarterly*, XXI (April, 1964), pp. 191–235. Cecelia M. Kenyon's "Alexander Hamilton: Rousseau of the Right," *Political Science Quarterly*, LXXIII (June, 1958), pp. 161–178, is a strikingly fresh approach to that controversial leader. Paul Goodman's piece, "Social Status of Party Leadership: The House of Representatives, 1797–1804," *William and Mary Quarterly*, XXV (July, 1968), pp. 465–474, contains interesting information on the leaders of both parties in the late 1790's. Norman K. Risjord, "The Virginia Federalists," *Journal of Southern History*, XXXIII (November, 1967), pp. 486–517, on the other hand, analyzes the followers of the Federalist party in Virginia and concludes that Beard's thesis that the Federalists represented the special class and financial interests which first appeared in the Federal Convention does not apply.

The biographical approach to the Federalists is particularly rich and rewarding. Washington's two terms are covered in the sixth volume of Douglas Southall Freeman's work, *George Washington: Patriot and President, 1784–1793* (New York, 1954), and in the seventh volume, *George Washington: First in Peace, 1793–1799* (New York, 1957), written by Freeman's research associates after his death, John Alexander Carroll and Mary Wells Ashworth. More penetrating comments about Washington's presidency, however, may be found in Marcus Cunliffe's brief but incisive *George Washington: Man and Monument* (Boston, 1958). The most definitive Hamilton biography is by Broadus Mitchell in two volumes: *Alexander Hamilton: Youth to Maturity, 1755–1788* (New York, 1957); and *Alexander Hamilton: The National Adventure, 1788–1804* (New York, 1962). Mitchell, well-grounded in economics, has the best explanation of Hamilton's fiscal program to appear in print. John C. Miller, *Alexander Hamilton: Portrait in Paradox* (New York, 1959), on the other hand, is more concerned with Hamilton's political philosophy. In recent years, John Adams has come to be viewed as a more representative exponent of Federalist thought than Ham-

ilton. Besides the book by Zoltan Haraszti, there are two other significant studies of Adam's political thought: John R. Howe's, *The Changing Political Thought of John Adams* (Princeton, 1966); and Edward Handler, *America and Europe in the Political Thought of John Adams* (Cambridge, 1964). Among the other Federalist leaders, five biographies are important for the light that they shed on the workings of the party: Samuel E. Morison's older version of *Life and Letters of Harrison Gray Otis, Federalist* (2 vols., Boston, 1913); Albert Beveridge, *The Life of John Marshall* (4 vols., Boston, 1916–1919); Winfred Bernhard, *Fisher Ames: Federalist and Statesman* (Chapel Hill, 1965); Morton Borden, *The Federalism of James A. Bayard* (New York, 1955); and Lynn Turner, *William Plumer of New Hampshire* (Chapel Hill, 1962).

The formation of the Federalist party and its political machinery has occupied the attention of many historians. Charles Beard's *Economic Origins of Jeffersonian Democracy* published in 1915 set the stage for a debate by claiming that the battle of the Federalists and Republicans in the 1800 election was nothing more than a continuation of the alignment of Federalist and Anti-Federalist forces that had appeared in the Constitutional Convention of 1787. Joseph Charles in his *Origins of American Party System* of 1956 challenged this thesis of political continuity and held that the Federalist party emerged largely out of the fight over Jay's Treaty. Older historians who had taken the view that the Federalists were centered solely in New England produced monographic studies such as Anson E. Morse's *Federalist Party in Massachusetts to the Year 1800* (Princeton, 1909), and Richard Purcell's, *Connecticut in Transition* (Washington, 1918). But recent historians have shown the Federalists had a much broader geographical base—Fischer's book, John A. Munroe's *Federalist Delaware, 1775–1815* (New Brunswick, 1954), and Lisle A. Rose's *Prologue to Democracy* (Lexington, 1968) being especially important on this theme. Scholars writing about the formation of the Jeffersonian Republican party on the national and state level often had much to say about the Federalist party in this same regard: see Noble E. Cunningham, Jr., *The Jeffersonian Republicans* (Chapel Hill, 1957); Marshall Smelser, *Democratic Republic, 1801–1815* (New York, 1968); Paul Goodman, *Democratic-Republicans of Massachusetts* (Cambridge, 1964); and Alfred F. Young, *Democratic Republicans of New York* (Chapel Hill, 1967).

Certain recent scholars have approached the subject of political parties and political development in the early Republic from an interdisciplinary point of view. For writings stressing political science concepts in the formation of both the Federalist and Jeffersonian parties, see William N. Chambers, *Political Parties in a New Nation* (New York, 1963); William N. Chambers, "Parties and Nation-Building in America," in Joseph LaPalombra and Myron Weiner, eds., *Political Parties and Political Development* (Princeton, 1966); and Paul Goodman, "The First American Party System," in William N. Chambers and Walter D. Burnham, eds., *The American Party Systems: Stages of Political Development* (New York, 1967). Social psychology is one conceptual tool employed by Richard Hofstadter in his *The Idea of a Party System* (Berkeley and Los Angeles, 1969). For the view of a sociologist who sought to compare the nation's early experiences with political parties with those of newly-emerging nation-states in modern times, see Seymour M. Lipset, *First New Nation* (New York, 1963). The works of Fischer, Kurtz, Dauer, and Rose mentioned previously also deal directly with the development of Federalist party machinery.

Federalist foreign policy likewise has been the subject of considerable controversy. Felix Gilbert, *To the Farewell Address* (Princeton, 1961), suggests that Federalists like Washington and Hamilton were motivated mainly by ideological considerations in framing foreign policy. Alexander DeConde, *Entangling Alliance* (Durham, 1958), on the other hand, claims the Federalist position on foreign affairs was the result of partisan and practical policies. Paul A. Varg, *Foreign Policy of the Founding Fathers* (East Lansing, 1963), finds that disagreement over America's commercial policy helped to bring about the formation of political parties. Bradford Perkins, *The First Rapprochement* (Philadelphia, 1955), presents a revisionist point of view of Anglo-American relations in the late 1790's. Two more traditional works by Samuel F. Bemis discuss the key treaties of the period: *Jay's Treaty* (New York, 1923); and *Pinckney's Treaty*, revised edition (New Haven, 1960).

Studies dealing with special aspects of the Federalist period are also significant. The Alien and Sedition Acts are treated in two books: James M. Smith, *Freedom's Fetters* (Ithaca, 1956); and John C. Miller, *Crisis in Freedom* (Boston, 1952). Leonard Levy in his *Legacy of Suppression* (Cambridge, 1960), shows the Federalists could not count on complete freedom of press and speech once Jefferson took office. Leonard White's *The Federalists* (New York, 1948), is the best book in the field of administrative history. For the connection between politics and the chartering of banks in the period, see Bray Hammond's *Banks and Politics in America from the Revolution to the Civil War* (Princeton, 1957). Russel B. Nye's *Cultural Life of the New Nation, 1776–1830* (New York, 1960), discusses the intellectual and cultural framework out of which the Federalists evolved.

Finally, no student should overlook certain works which do not deal explicitly with the Federalists, but discuss them within a broader sweep of history. Among the older works, De Tocqueville's classic, *Democracy in America*, available in many editions, still contains some brilliant insights. Of the recent books, the following will prove profitable: Louis Hartz, *Liberal Tradition in America* (New York, 1955); Daniel J. Boorstin, *The Americans: The National Experience* (New York, 1966); and Robert R. Palmer, *Age of the Democratic Revolution*, 2 vols. (Princeton, 1959 and 1964).